"When it comes to giving, Jean Shafiroff leads the pack. To anyone who wants to fundraise, volunteer, or show support by giving, I must stress: Do not keep this book on your bookshelf. Place it on your desk. It should be your bible, your roadmap to success in the world of philanthropy."

—ELSIE MCCABE THOMPSON, President, New York City Mission Society

"Jean Shafiroff's vision for philanthropy, as outlined in this book and carried out in her own life, is one of collaboration, authenticity, and respect. She sets forth a path for philanthropists, new and old, to reflect on their values and discover their own philanthropic identity. As a true reflection of its author, this book embodies a spirit of fierce commitment and dedication to causes greater than one's self."

—ANA OLIVEIRA, President and CEO, The New York Women's Foundation

"*Successful Philanthropy* is a call to action to each of us to give back to our communities. It is both a pleasure and an inspiration to read definitions of being a philanthropist and the heartfelt gift of giving, and the manner in which we can all help. Whether in small or bountiful ways, we can all engage in philanthropy. As an engaged and dedicated Board Member of French Heritage Society, Jean epitomizes the values of a true philanthropist; she is generous, caring, concerned, and determined. With this same passion, she has written a book that is both inspiring but also equally practical in its detailed explanation of how individual philanthropy can be understood and pursued by each of us. I am sure, with the admirable new modern interest in philanthropy, that this book will be appreciated by many, and serve as an inspiration to others."

—ELIZABETH F. STRIBLING, Chairman, French Heritage Society

"Jean Shafiroff is a force of nature. She is one of the most passionate and compassionate donors that I know. In this handy, easy-to-read volume, she lays out everything a budding philanthropist needs to know to get started, to make smart decisions and, ultimately, to make an impact in the world through philanthropy. I recommend it."

—DAVID RIVEL, CEO, Jewish Board of Family & Children's Services

"To understand philanthropy you can either read Jean Shafiroff's book or you can simply experience Jean Shafiroff. I am fortunate to have done both. While the etymology of the concept of 'Doing well by doing good' is often attributed to Benjamin Franklin, the behavior is quintessential Jean Shafiroff. She evokes the true spirit of giving, philanthropy, and volunteerism every day of her life in her passion for and service to important causes and organizations."

—STEVEN M. BERNSTEIN, President,
Southampton Hospital Foundation

"*Successful Philanthropy* is both a passionate call to action for philanthropists and an invaluable manifesto for all of us who endeavor to make a difference in the not-for-profit community by giving of our time, talent, and financial resources. Scarcely a philosophical treatise, Jean Shafiroff's book is a pragmatic guide to giving that is modeled on her own remarkable life experience as a successful philanthropist and volunteer."

—ROBERT S. CHALONER, President
and CEO, Southampton Hospital

"Jean's 'call to action' derives from her generous spirit and compelling interest in making the world a better place. Taking a serious, fresh look at giving, she is both a skilled mentor and an inspiration."

—ROBERT FERGUSON, Vice President for Development, Fashion Institute of Technology

"Philanthropy entails the giving of one's time, one's resources, and of oneself. Having worked successfully with Jean Shafiroff on behalf of the Southampton Animal Shelter Foundation, her knowledge and dedication in the field is highly respected. The reader will benefit from Jean's extensive experience that is found in her book."

—JONATHAN W. McCANN, Board President, Southampton Animal Shelter Foundation

AN INSPIRATIONAL AND PRACTICAL
GUIDE TO GIVING

SUCCESSFUL PHILANTHROPY

HOW TO MAKE A LIFE BY WHAT YOU GIVE

JEAN SHAFIROFF

INTRODUCTION BY
GEORGINA BLOOMBERG

Hatherleigh Press is committed to preserving and protecting the
natural resources of the earth. Environmentally responsible and
sustainable practices are embraced within the company's
mission statement.

Visit us at www.hatherleighpress.com and register online
for free offers, discounts, special events, and more.

Successful Philanthropy

Library of Congress Cataloging-in-Publication Data is available
upon request.
ISBN: 978-1-57826-617-3

Cover and Interior Design by Carolyn Kasper
Cover Photograph by Gregory Partanio

Printed in the United States
10 9 8 7 6 5 4 3 2 1

33614059718972

CONTENTS

4

HOW TO CHOOSE A CHARITY 101

5

HOW TO TREAT VOLUNTEERS, PAID EMPLOYEES, THOSE SERVICED BY A CHARITY, AND DONORS 137

COMMUNITIES BUILT ON GIVING: MODELS FOR SOCIAL PHILANTHROPY 173

FOREWORD
Scott Elkins

F OR MORE THAN 20 years I have worked in philanthropy and with many esteemed charities including Carnegie Hall, Cambridge University, Royal Hospital Chelsea, Helen Bamber Foundation, Margaret Thatcher Foundation, and today the Margaret Thatcher Scholarship Trust at Somerville College, Oxford University, amongst others.

"Helping to bring about change" is a personal mantra that I repeatedly state. It is a belief that I know Jean Shafiroff shares and wishes to convey to all through her book. I have spent the last two decades working with fiscal benefactions, which is important and essential in our world. Jean is correct when she states that everyone can be a philanthropist in the new millennium. This is a message that I hope all embrace, realizing there are many ways we all can help.

On a personal level, I have had a disease—multiple sclerosis—for more than 15 years. Days ago I sat down with an 11-year-old who has multiple sclerosis and is suffering tremendously.

I tried to cheer this young child on to fight and work on all levels; call or visit anytime if I can help further. My fourth grade son in response would also ask his school if they would hold an awareness and fundraiser in support of MS—for a fee of $3 that goes to a MS charity, all students can dress casual instead of wearing the school uniform. I was touched by my son's personal and instant response; a relatively small amount of support though on a very meaningful scale.

Humanity, legacy, philanthropy. These are all words I have heard Jean use often and I find moving. My favorite quote from Sir Winston Churchill remains: "we make a living by what we get, we make a life by what we give."

Successful Philanthropy is an excellent book and valuable resource for all. I salute Jean for encouraging us to give back to those in need any way that we can: volunteering, sharing skills, giving money, and equally offering other resources we have to improve our communities. *Successful Philanthropy* is a road map on how to start becoming a philanthropist, a guide to help change the world for all, and a reflection on the incredible symbiotic benefit to giving. Thank you, Jean, for this book and your impressive thoughts and hopes for current and future generations.

With kindest wishes,
Scott Elkins
US Campaign Director, Margaret Thatcher
Scholarship Trust at Oxford University
CEO, SE Advisors
Person living with MS

INTRODUCTION
Georgina Bloomberg

ARAH WAS MY first friend at NYU. Our worlds collided one day over lunch at a small deli on Astor Place. The impact was so strong that years after losing touch, I still recognize her as the most influential person I have ever crossed paths with.

Sarah and I shared the same love for horses. She had grown up in a small town and bartered with her local stable; she did the dirty work—hours of mucking stalls, cleaning tack, and other jobs around the barn—in exchange for the occasional lesson. When I asked her why she wasn't trying out for our NYU equestrian team, she told me she would love nothing more and, in fact, that had always been her dream: to ride for a college team and launch a career around horses. But for Sarah, this wasn't a realistic goal, as she simply couldn't afford the proper clothing and equipment that one needs to ride. As anyone lucky enough to take a seat atop this majestic creature knows, riding a horse can be an expensive sport; one cannot do it safely without, at minimum, boots or chaps to protect one's legs and a helmet to protect one's head. To ride in an interscholastic program, one must also factor in that clothing and equipment be competition worthy, a designation that can cost hundreds of dollars. I don't remember anything before or after that lunchtime exchange…the wheels in my head had started turning instantaneously.

Years before, I had been cleaning out a closet in my father's home and found some old riding attire that I had worn growing up. As I am the youngest in my family, the clothes were only lightly used and had simply been outgrown. But as I sifted through boots, britches, and show coats, I realized that I had no idea what to do with any of it; there was simply nowhere to donate riding clothing. Instead of packing everything up, I simply put the pile back into the closet and forgot about it until that fateful moment with Sarah when my mind went reeling back to that pile in my childhood closet. It was then that I realized Sarah wasn't the only kid in this predicament, and suddenly two dots that needed to be connected were right before my eyes.

In go-mode, I called up a contact in a prominent riding association and told him to get the word out to as many schools as possible that I was collecting clothing and equipment to send to any school in need. I had no plan, no real concept, but I made the decision that I could make a difference and help people. It was my duty to figure the rest out. I began asking fellow riders at horse shows and soon enough, everyone who heard started dropping off boxes full of items that had been shoved into the back of closets for years on end. I even received horse blankets that I was able to donate to rescues to keep horses warm for the winters! I organized everything myself in my mother's garage, sending boxes out free of charge whenever someone wrote me a request. Soon, her garage was housing so many items that her car was forced out! I started getting letters from therapeutic riding programs and individuals who heard about the colleges I had been able to help and asked to be recipients of the items as well. It was a full-fledged operation!

Fast forward 10 years and The Rider's Closet, the organization I founded as a result of this fateful meal with Sarah, collects thousands of pieces of clothing and equipment every year for intercollegiate and therapeutic programs, as well as any individual person in need. It is run through Pegasus Therapeutic Riding by its incredible staff and volunteers and has grown into something that is helping more people than I ever could have dreamed of to stay with the sport they love. The Rider's Closet has aided children who could not afford a therapeutic riding program without proper equipment, college riders who dare to follow their dreams, and those who partake in every level of the sport in being able to afford to be comfortable and safe, two things that should not be a luxury. We send items completely free of charge all over the country, and have clothed everyone from a child with disabilities making huge advances at a therapeutic riding program to a junior national equitation champion. I receive letters every week from riders who tell me that they wouldn't have been able to stay in the sport or around horses had they not received the assistance this program provided.

Making life a little easier for people who love this sport as much as I do literally makes me jump for joy. It's my way of giving back to a community that has given so much to me throughout the years. Moreover, this program is vital to what I have learned about philanthropy: both donors and doers are crucial and we can all make a difference. Although I am extremely lucky to be in a position to contribute financially to causes that I care about, it is the contribution of creative resources and time that can often add the most value to others. My heart swells during the countless hours volunteering, be it at homeless shelters, animal rescues, or holiday kid's programs. Although I acknowledge that money is required to keep programs up and running, monetary donations do not a philanthropist make; being generous of spirit will never be overshadowed by being generous with a checkbook. For me, philanthropy is about discovering the satisfaction and deep sense of fulfillment that is a direct result of helping those in need. I saw a void and I found a way to help fill it. Don't ever think that you can't help make the world a better place just because you can't write a check. If you see someone in need of something and you think you can help, go do it. You never know what that initial idea will grow into or how many people you will end up helping as a result.

—Georgina Bloomberg

PHILANTHROPY

: good will to fellow members of the human race; *especially* : active effort to promote human welfare

2

a : an act or gift done or made for humanitarian purposes

b : an organization distributing or supported by funds set aside for humanitarian purposes

HOW TO START

"Since the world has existed, there has been injustice. But it is one world, the more so as it becomes smaller, more accessible. There is no question that there is a moral obligation that those who have should give to those who have nothing."

—AUDREY HEPBURN

T HIS BOOK OFFERS you many different
ways to start.

**Begin with the person most important to
starting it all: you.** *You* can become a philanthropist. Philanthropy entails giving time or
financial contributions to improve the lives of
people and our world. Philanthropy can also
encompass giving to improve the environment
or to protect the animals that cannot help
themselves. A philanthropist is defined as "one
who makes an active effort to promote human
welfare: a person who practices *philanthropy.*"

Describing yourself as a philanthropist may
seem odd at first. For some people, being a
philanthropist sounds like something limited
only to those who give large financial gifts. But
the truth is that philanthropy is accessible to
anyone.

No matter what you do or how much you
earn, you can become a philanthropist. In these
pages, you will learn what being a philanthropist

means and why a new definition of "philanthropist" is so vital to the future of our society, the human race, and the world.

Start by discovering your interests and passions. Finding what moves you will make your journey of giving far more exciting. Once you have discovered your passions, your desire to affect change will become all that much easier. Your participation will have far more meaning. This book will help you ask the right questions so that you can discover your goals as they relate to philanthropy.

Start by asking meaningful questions. Life moves so fast that we often forget to think about the power of giving in our lives.

This book invites you to take the time to really think about the role that giving plays in your life. It offers you the opportunity to ask yourself: What have you been given? What do you want to give back to others and to the world?

Once you begin to explore your own personal

reasons for giving, you can develop strategies for incorporating giving into your busy life. Giving can be far more rewarding than you can imagine.

A note: the portions of this book that discuss *why* we should give are not meant to tell you what causes you should become involved with. They are meant to give you the tools to discover the answers for yourself. The content in this book is meant to reawaken thoughts and feelings you might already have, invite new perspectives, and welcome you to consider new reasons for personal giving.

Start with your story. You can be the author of your unique story of giving. Each person chooses his or her own path as a philanthropist. Giving can change to your ever-changing life circumstances.

This book provides suggestions for getting started: tips, ideas, and strategies. Adapt these guidelines to your own life, based on how you decide to give—whether by volunteering time, sharing knowledge, and/or donating financial resources.

Helping to create positive change requires some idea of how you might want to help. Identify the causes you care about most, learn what will be required of you, and finally choose the charity (or charities) that are the best fit for you.

Start with what matters in the end. Through giving, we become more fulfilled human beings. We learn more about ourselves and the change we can help create in the world. We can achieve the satisfaction of knowing that we contributed to lasting effects that will endure beyond our lifetime.

Start now. Real change requires action. Each one of us plays a role in society's movement forward.

Now is the time for all of us to do what we can.

There are many valuable nonprofit organizations working hard to solve problems in our cities and towns, across America and across the globe. However, as hard as these organizations work, and as passionate and committed as they are to their cause, they cannot do it alone. Enormous demands are placed upon the groups who help those in need and who strive to improve societal conditions. In order for these organizations to succeed, we must all contribute.

We cannot put off giving indefinitely. We must all try to do something. The time to get involved is now!

We should all be asking ourselves these questions:

- When we leave this world, what did we do?
- Did we leave anything of value to humanity?
- Were we a part of the movement to affect change?
- Did we follow our passions, letting them lead us to take action?

The invitation for us to give back is there, every day. It provides us with the opportunity to share with others and with the world. It offers us a choice—the most significant choice we face in our lifetime: to live with blinders on, ignoring the suffering and needs around us, or to step up and take action.

All we have to do is accept: to say yes to the chance to be a philanthropist and make giving a part of our lives.

"Be the change you wish to see in the world."

—Mahatma Gandhi

1

A NEW DEFINITION
OF PHILANTHROPY

"I am of the opinion that my life belongs to the community. And as long as I live, it is my privilege to do for it whatever I can. I want to be thoroughly used up when I die, for the harder I work, the more I live. Life is no brief candle to me; it is a sort of splendid torch, which I have got hold of for a short moment, and I want to make it burn as brightly as possible before handing it on to the future generations."

—George Bernard Shaw

TRUE FULFILLMENT, THE feeling of being satisfied not only with your world but the role you play in it, can be achieved through embracing the spirit of giving. It is through giving and caring for others that we understand our role and purpose in life. This is a truth known to the greatest minds of our generation and the generations that have come before us.

Throughout history, those who have made the most lasting positive influence on society are those who made giving back a priority in their lives.

They were committed to putting the needs of others before their own. They had the courage to speak out—and to transform their words into action. To the best of their ability and in whatever way they were most capable, they dedicated their lives to the betterment of humanity.

Today, the legacy of these men and women lives on. Their stories continue to inspire us.

Their lessons continue to teach us. Their voices continue to motivate us. They invite us to write our own legacy of giving through personal acts of philanthropy.

NOTABLE PHILANTHROPISTS

BILL GATES

Bill Gates, co-founder of Microsoft, gives back through the Bill & Melinda Gates Foundation, the largest private foundation in the world. The Foundation supports causes that promote global healthcare and reduce extreme poverty. In the United States, the Foundation advances educational opportunities and access to information technology.

THE GATES-BUFFET GIVING PLEDGE

In 2010, Warren Buffet with Bill and Melinda Gates started The Giving Pledge to encourage the wealthiest individuals in the world to commit to giving the bulk of their wealth to charity. Gates and Buffet themselves pledged to donate at least 50% of their wealth to charity. As of 2015, over 100 billionaires have committed to giving at least half of their wealth to philanthropic causes. Those involved in the pledge include Facebook CEO Mark Zuckerberg, Hollywood director George Lucas, Home Depot co-founder Arthur Blank, Spanx inventor Sara Blakely, and the Rockefeller family.

WARREN BUFFET

Known as the most successful investor of the 20th century, Warren Buffet has pledged to give 99% of his wealth to charity, much of this through the Bill & Melinda Gates Foundation. In the past, Buffet has also raised funds for Girls, Inc. and the Glide Foundation. In 2010,

Buffett, along with Bill Gates, launched The Giving Pledge.

MICHAEL BLOOMBERG

Michael Bloomberg has said, "The thing about great wealth is that you can't take it with you." A man of his word, Michael Bloomberg often shares his plan to give his wealth away. A business magnate and former Mayor of New York City, Michael Bloomberg gives back (through his Bloomberg Philanthropies) to causes in the areas of the arts, education, the environment, government innovation, and public health located in New York City, across the country, and around the world. Michael Bloomberg has given over $3 billion to an array of causes; in 2013, Bloomberg Philanthropies made donations totaling over $450 million. Its unique approach to philanthropy comes from Michael Bloomberg's experience serving as New York City's mayor for 12 years, as well as his experience running the multi-billion dollar company that he created.

Michael Bloomberg's passion for philanthropy and his strong desire to improve the lives of others by creating societal change first began as a child. He learned his values from his parents and from his experiences as an Eagle Scout. His first donation was a $5 check, made out to his college's alumni association. This was given immediately after graduating in appreciation of the education he received. At that time this was all he could afford. Today, his checks to charity are much larger, but they come with the same idea in mind. Michael Bloomberg firmly believes that you should give what you can, and he has followed this principle throughout his life. Michael Bloomberg has given more than $1 billion to Johns Hopkins and its public health facility—the largest in the U.S. In recognition of his extraordinary generosity, Johns Hopkins has named its public health school the Bloomberg School of Public Health, in his honor.

THE FORD FAMILY/ THE FORD FOUNDATION

Founded with an initial gift from Edsel Ford, son of Henry Ford, in 1936, the Ford Foundation is dedicated to advancing human welfare in the areas of educational opportunity, human rights, economic fairness, democracy, health, affordable housing, sustainable development, and the creative arts through its numerous grant programs. The Ford Foundation is the second largest private foundation in the United States, with an endowment of over $10 billion.

JOHN D. ROCKEFELLER/ THE ROCKEFELLER FOUNDATION

John D. Rockefeller founded the Rockefeller Foundation with his son in 1913 in New York. Over the past century, its central mission has been "to promote the well-being of humanity throughout the world." It supports causes in the areas of unrestricted access to education for all; as well as health and hygiene, including funds to construct and endow the Johns Hopkins School of Public Health in 1916 and support studies at the Harvard School of Public Health.

WHAT IS PHILANTHROPY?

Philanthropy shapes our future, our children's future, and our world's future. It also offers us the opportunity to feel personally and genuinely fulfilled. Yet the word "philanthropy" is not really a part of our everyday vocabulary. So then, what exactly *is* philanthropy?

Rooted in the Greek *philanthrōpos*, which combines the word "philos" (loving) and "anthropos" ("human being" or "humanity"), *philanthropy* literally means "love of humanity." In essence, philanthropy means directing the vital, life-changing force of love towards our fellow man.

At the heart of philanthropy is an understanding of how our humanity, our "humanness," binds us together. Our humanity connects us, in spite of cultural differences or language barriers. It joins us, across the miles and over the oceans that separate us. No matter how different we may seem from the outside—how unalike our life's circumstances, appearance, or personal preferences are—we all know what it means to be human. We are all intimately familiar with life's challenges, triumphs, joys, and struggles. Each one of us knows the pride of accomplishment and achievement. We all know what it means to feel loved, to be part of a community, family, or partnership.

We also know how hard it can be to feel alone, separated, and different from everyone else. We know how quickly circumstances can change and take an unexpected turn from promising to hopeless—and how desperate, afraid, and alone we feel when it seems as if our lives are falling apart.

Being human links us to each other. It makes us brothers and sisters, no matter how different our life circumstances may be. Through philanthropy, we embrace these common human bonds. Philanthropy offers new perspectives and the ability to reach outside of ourselves.

Our destiny is *not* to go through life alone—competing, fighting, and toiling in a struggle to meet our own personal needs and wants. Our destiny is to do our part, giving back to a world that desperately needs us. Philanthropy invites us to direct the course of our lives along a path to something better, bigger, and more meaningful.

PHILANTHROPY AND PHILANTHROPISTS: NEW DEFINITIONS

A philanthropist is defined as: "one who makes an active effort to promote human welfare: a person who practices *philanthropy.*" Often, when we speak about philanthropists, it is in the context of big-name givers—those who are very wealthy and who have ample funds to give.

In truth, we can *all* be philanthropists. The modern definition casts aside the notion that only the wealthy can be philanthropists. Here, defined on these pages, is a new and modern definition of philanthropy. Being a philanthropist is attainable to all.

This new definition of philanthropy means that each and every one of us can become a philanthropist: practicing philanthropy means acting out of a love for humanity, in any number of ways. It means we can follow our passions to help our world and all those in it.

Theodore Roosevelt said, "Do what you can, with what you have, where you are." This applies perfectly to philanthropy. Give what you can, whether it means donating finances, time as a volunteer, or sharing your skills and knowledge. All of these gifts are incredibly valuable and define you as a philanthropist.

Philanthropy can mean helping our world directly or helping to preserve it for future generations. **The Reverend Mae "Mother" Wyatt said, "When we plant a tree, we don't plant it for ourselves, but for our children."** The actions we take now as philanthropists ensure the well-being of future generations.

Most of us participate in acts of philanthropy every day or certainly every week. If you made the effort to reach out to someone in need by lending emotional support or showing kindness to a stranger in need, you are beginning your journey as a philanthropist. You might want to write down on paper the ways in which you have participated as a philanthropist. Reflecting on the many different ways you can do more to help others will help you reach higher goals. Create a list of the activities that you would like to participate in to achieve your goal of becoming a philanthropist. This is a step by step process. No one will judge you. You can create your own path!

Remember, philanthropy invites us to reach outside of ourselves in an effort to help others, and to live to our ultimate potential as human beings.

PHILANTHROPY IS ...

- **Passion:** A passion and desire to create change in the world.

- **Commitment:** A commitment to do our part to prevent and reduce the suffering of those around us.

- **Understanding:** An understanding that no matter how different we may seem from one another, we all need to support each other during challenging times.

- **Respect:** A respect for the thread of life and humanity that binds us.

- **Action:** A decision to take action and make something we believe in happen.

PHILANTHROPY: AN AMERICAN VALUE

The value of philanthropy is woven into the very fabric of the United States and the American way of life.

The founders of this country, men and women who had left their homelands behind to start a new life based on freedom, were brave individuals who believed in independence. Yet they also knew that they had to build their future on shared resources. This required that each citizen devote him or herself to strengthening their community. Three of the colonies formed in the 1600s by the colonists (Massachusetts, Pennsylvania, and Virginia) were known as "commonwealths": literally, "common wealth," an ideal society where everyone contributed to the common resources or "wealth."

Our forefathers knew the value of coming together for the greater good. They foresaw an America built on strong communities made up of committed citizens.

GIVING AND RELIGION

Many religions count giving as one of their core values.

The Christian Bible says, "it is more blessed to give than to receive." Charitable giving is an important part of being a Christian, a way to honor a giving God. Giving back through charitable works is seen as a way to do God's will on earth, and to get closer to an understanding of God as a force of love.

Likewise, an important tenet of Judaism is "tzedakah," a Hebrew word which means righteousness, fairness, or justice. Under tzedakah, giving is both a responsibility and a duty, an act committed to further justice. It encompasses helping the poor and needy as well as other worthy causes, through monetary donations, direct aid, and other forms of assistance. But the highest level of giving, according to tzedakah, is actually helping someone to become self-sufficient.

The notion of giving is built into one of the five pillars of Islam: *zakat*, a form of obligatory giving of alms, considered a religious tax for Muslims only. Zakat is taken as a percentage based on one's income, savings, and wealth. Zakat roughly translates as "that which purifies" and is considered a means to purify a person's income and wealth.

In Hinduism, generosity, charity, or giving is known as *dana*. Dana is an important aspect of *dharma* (religious duty or conduct towards all living things). The Bhagavadgita, a sacred Hindu text, discusses the types of giving and emphasizes that giving without any expectation of appreciation or reward is the only type of giving that is beneficial to both the giver and the receiver; if giving is motivated by selfishness, it does not have spiritual value. True enjoyment and peace lies in a detachment from wealth and ownership.

In Buddhism, giving with pure motivation is called *dana paramita* (Sanskrit), or *dana parami* (Pali), meaning "perfection of giving." In giving, there should be no expectation of reward or recognition. Giving is seen as a basic human virtue that communicates the depth of a person's humanity. In the teachings of the Buddha, giving is a vital part of spiritual development.

PHILANTHROPY:
A CALL TO ACTION

Philanthropy is not an exclusive club. It is open to all. Being a philanthropist is not the sole responsibility of a few people "at the top" who can make large financial gifts. For as large as the biggest financial gifts may be, they are just the beginning. They may fuel existing projects or the initiations of new projects, but they can't do everything.

The simple truth is those gifts alone cannot bring about lasting change. Gifts of all sizes are needed. Whether a gift is large or small, it brings us one step closer to a bigger goal. It also provides a catalyst to more giving. When we all work towards a common goal, we can achieve far more than if just a small percentage of the population is involved.

Philanthropy is not just about giving a monetary gift. Our gifts of time, attention, knowledge, and experience are all very valuable.

There are countless ways we can give: we can volunteer at a soup kitchen, help to fundraise, or assist by tutoring students, just to name a few. All of our gifts are valuable—our technical skills, job-related know-how, and work experience can make us valuable contributors.

CHANGE THROUGH PHILANTHROPY IS WITHIN REACH

We live at a time when great change is possible, more so than ever before. We live in an era of philanthropic giving that the generations who came before us could not have possibly dreamed of.

Because of recent technological advances and scientific discoveries, we are nearer than ever to solving some of the world's problems. We are closer to lessening poverty, reducing hunger, fighting disease, and improving education.

Technology has also made the world a smaller, more connected place. The barriers of distance across the country and around the globe are disappearing. The ability to connect to people throughout the world through various forms of media allows us to work with one another to solve global problems. The internet, cell phones, and social media enable us to reach more and more people. Interactive communication informs us of problems we might otherwise not have known about.

DURING HURRICANE SANDY, it was our extensive media capabilities that first informed us about the disaster. We were able to quickly learn where our help was needed most. With this knowledge, we then worked towards solving the extensive problems caused by the hurricane.

Our connectedness and globalization through media makes it possible to learn of problems that might be afflicting thousands of people in remote places. And because we have this knowledge, we can do something about it—we can take action and work on solving serious problems.

"Life's persistent and most urgent question is 'What are you doing for others?'"

—MARTIN LUTHER KING, JR.

2

WHY SHOULD
I GIVE?

"Everyone can be great, because everyone can serve."

—Dr. Martin Luther King, Jr.

THE ROOTS OF PHILANTHROPY draw from a mighty wellspring: the spirit of giving.

Giving is truly powerful. Through giving, our resources multiply exponentially.

When we spend our time serving others, our efforts and personal attention have the power to heal.

When we share our knowledge, skills, or expertise with someone in need, we empower an individual to open new doors on his or her own.

When we make a financial gift, our monetary donation is transformed from currency into hope, opportunity, and change for those who need it the most.

Through giving time, knowledge, and/or monetary resources, we give those in need the means to improve their lives. When our gifts are received by others, what we possess blossoms ten-, twenty-, 100-fold.

THE GIFT OF GIVING

The ability to give is a remarkable gift in and of itself. It is a blessing unlike any other. No matter who we are, where we come from, or what kind of financial resources we have, we can all offer something meaningful. Giving is a privilege bestowed on all of us.

The way we give—what we give, how much we give, and how often—may be different for each one of us, yet all gifts are vitally important. Each gift sustains the life-affirming cycle of philanthropy.

And our ability to give can grow even *stronger* as we age. Often, as we get older, we become rich in the experience and knowledge that makes our own personal perspective a valuable gift to others. Many retirees have an abundance of available time and resources to give. Retirees who volunteer often discover a great way to spend their time and build upon the foundation of a meaningful life. This is not the case for everyone, but the older we are (provided we are still in good health), the more experience, resources, and wisdom we most likely will have to share.

The spirit of giving stays with us, always. It is there as the years pass; it may evolve as our available resources change, but it never disappears. It is a part of who we are for our entire lifetime.

Giving strengthens us. It broadens our capabilities. It helps us to grow. There isn't anything else quite like it that we can offer, possess, or obtain. The ability to give is a true gift—the greatest gift of all.

"The raising of extraordinarily large sums of money, given voluntarily and freely by millions of our fellow Americans, is a unique American tradition... Philanthropy, charity, giving voluntarily and freely... call it what you like, but it is truly a jewel of an American tradition."

—JOHN F. KENNEDY

GIVING IN AMERICA TODAY

Giving has always been an important priority for Americans. This has been true even in difficult economic times. When times are toughest, it is often those with more resources who feel compelled to take action by giving time or money.

Since the recession ended in mid-2009, statistics on charitable giving have been steadily on the rise, showing that Americans consider giving to be a top priority. In 2013—which marked the fourth straight year of a *rise* in giving—Americans made gifts totaling an estimated $335 billion. Of note is the fact that between 2011 and 2013 it was individuals, not corporations, who gave the most: 73 percent of the rise in total giving during that period was due to individual Americans, families, and households deciding to give back to help those still in need.

On the global stage, the United States stands out for its commitment to a full spectrum of charitable giving. According to the World Giving Index's 2014 study, which involved 135 countries around the world over a five-year period (2009-2013), the United States was the only country to land in the Top 10 for all three categories of giving behavior covered by the study: helping a stranger, volunteering time, and making monetary donations.

We are an incredible resource. In 2014, the population of the United States rose to over 318 million. If each one of those 318 million people wove giving into their lives every day, in some way, the impact on our nation and the world at large would be nothing short of amazing.

The American people's commitment to giving is something we should be proud of...and each one of us should continue the work that those before us have started.

WHY DO WE GIVE?

There are a multitude of reasons why we give. Giving stems from a passion and desire to be part of positive change.

Sometimes, giving is an important part of our faith or spiritual practice. Other times we may simply feel compelled to give, out of a belief that it is the right thing to do. For many of us, charitable giving is woven into our upbringing as a basic value.

There are other, more general reasons why we give. It might be helpful to create your own list of reasons that compel you to get involved as a philanthropist. You may wish to create a personal journal or write down a list of reasons that compel you to act. Or, you may want to start a conversation with a friend or loved one about what interests you most. There are several different steps you can take to begin thinking about the role of philanthropy in your life.

RELIGIOUS CHARITIES

Across the world, many charities connected to religious groups assist in aiding the poor and working in a variety of ways to better the lives of the underserved. Many of these charities work for all people, regardless of the religious background of the people they serve.

For example, Catholic Charities Agencies across America help people in need and serve communities in outreach and service that are part of active efforts to share the love of Christ. With over 160 member agencies in the United States, Catholic Charities serves the needs of over 2,600 different locations. The mission of Catholic Charities Agencies is to provide service to people in need, to advocate for justice in social structures, and to call the entire church and other people of goodwill to do the same.

For over a century, the Jewish Board of Family and Children's Services (also known as The Jewish Board) has been helping New Yorkers by addressing and promoting betterment in all aspects of an individual's life, including mental and physical health, family, housing, employment, and education. The Jewish Board is the largest social service charity in New York and serves more than 43,000 New Yorkers from all religious, ethnic, and socioeconomic backgrounds each year.

Joel Osteen Ministries gives food, clothing, and medical supplies to many of those in need around the world. Joel Osteen, a world famous Christian preacher in over 100 countries, uses television, the internet, podcasts, and other modern means of communication to reach others with inspiring messages of hope, personal empowerment, and celebration of unconditional love rooted in the Bible.

Here are several reasons that may resonate with you.

We give because we are passionate about a cause. At the core of philanthropy is a *passion to help others and a desire to be involved in the process*. This passion fuels philanthropy and builds a solid foundation for our charitable work. But where does this passion come from?

Passion about a cause can be motivated by a personal experience or tragedy. The mother of a child who suffers with autism may be passionate about not wanting to see others suffer with the condition. As a result, she becomes involved with a nonprofit whose mission is to cure autism.

Passion for a cause can also be fueled by a love of the arts. A passionate art collector may wish to share this love with others by donating works of art or by even financing a wing of a museum.

For example, Leonard Lauder, a passionate philanthropist and lover of the arts, saw that the Metropolitan Museum of Art (also known as the MET) in New York City which possesses some of the finest art in the world, lacked a strong Cubist collection. Leonard Lauder decided to donate his large collection of Cubist Art, valued in excess of $1 billion, to the MET. He has also promised to give additional works of Cubist Art to the MET in the future. Mr. Lauder saw a need that had to be filled and gave very generously. The Metropolitan Museum of Art and those who visit it will always benefit from Leonard Lauder's generous gift. Leonard Lauder was involved in philanthropic giving long before his gift to the Metropolitan Museum Art. In 2008, he donated over $100 million to the Whitney Art Museum to assure its long-term sustainability. Mr. Lauder has also demonstrated his philanthropic nature in other areas besides art. He is the Co-Founder and Chairman of the Alzheimer's Drug Discovery Foundation and a member of the President's Council of Memorial

Sloan-Kettering Hospital. Mr. Lauder and his late wife, Evelyn, were also actively involved in the creation of the Evelyn H. Lauder Breast Center at the Memorial Sloan-Kettering Cancer Center in New York.

John Alfred Paulson, one of America's most successful and prominent hedge fund managers, saw a need for a stronger engineering school at Harvard University and in June of 2015 decided to donate $400 million to Harvard University's School of Engineering and Applied Sciences, causing the school to be renamed the Harvard John A. Paulson School of Engineering and Applied Sciences. A graduate of Harvard Business School, John wanted to show his appreciation and did so by giving Harvard University the largest gift that it had ever received. In 2012, observing a need for improvements in Central Park in New York City, Mr. Paulson donated $100 million to Central Park Conservancy. In addition, Mr. Paulson has made large contributions to a variety of other causes ranging from healthcare to public education—always where he saw a need!

Stephen A. Schwarzman, Chairman and CEO of Blackstone Group, a private equity and financial advisory firm, is ranked by Forbes as one of the wealthiest men in America. Mr. Schwarzman has shown his passion for furthering educational opportunities through his generous philanthropic giving. In 2008, Mr. Schwarzman donated $100 million toward the expansion of the New York Public Library. Then in April of 2013, he gave a $100 million personal gift to establish and endow a scholarship program in China. More recently in 2015, he announced a $150 million gift to fund a campus center at Yale University named the Schwarzman Center. In September 2015, he and his wife Christine Schwarzman announced a $40 million gift to help underprivileged students pay for Catholic education. This gift coincided with Pope Francis's trip to the United States.

We give because we know the actions and choices made now can help in the future. With every decision we make, we plant the seeds for future generations. Acting recklessly has consequences for those who come after us; for our earth and environment, as well as our communities, towns, and cities. Therefore, we must act with consideration for our children and our children's children: they deserve to lead fulfilling lives and look forward to a bright future. We can provide for their future by donating time and resources to educational institutions and other groups that focus on the well-being of those who follow us.

We give because small gifts can help lead to big change. Although a single gift may be small, it can still have great impact. A life can be changed with a handful of loose pocket change. Inspiration can be sparked by a single book donated to a local library. Many small gifts together have the power to change everything, one step at a time. If each one of us gave up the equivalent of the cost of one cup of coffee, *$220 billion more* could go to charity—in just one year! In short, a lot of little changes can add up to real impact.

We give because we are compelled to take action. Certain issues may be so important to us that we feel that the time for us to step in and take action is *now*. We may give to a cause we believe in by sharing our financial resources or time to ensure that an issue we feel strongly about receives the help that it needs. It may feel wrong to just stand idly by while a policy that we disagree with goes unchallenged, or an injustice goes unquestioned. Strong feelings can compel us to step off the sidelines and take action.

We give because giving honors life and the power of the human spirit to affect change. Giving allows us to be part of a collective process of change. When we work together with others in support of a cause we care about, we also become enriched by the work. Working with others, meeting new people and turning strangers into friends, can connect us to each other and elevate our spirit. Giving can be a celebration of life—a celebration of how much each one of us has to offer, how much a group of people can transform circumstances for the better, and how much good we can do when we choose to participate.

We give because it makes good use of our abilities and taps into what we have to offer. Giving awakens parts of ourselves that we may have lost touch with—parts that are valuable to other people and helpful to the world.

We give because it is part of our upbringing and culture. We believe that access to all of life's opportunities is what makes life worth living. As members of a community, we stand up for each other. We take action when we witness suffering. When we hear that children in different parts of the world are going through their days with empty stomachs and that their classrooms do not have textbooks, we are saddened. This moves us to action, to work to bring about change.

We know that giving benefits us all. Education moves a nation forward. Sharing with one another is part of our culture; making resources available to all benefits everyone. Each one of us holds the keys to the future; when we help each other, we act to benefit society at large and humanity in general.

We give because we do not want to see suffering and we wish to assuage it. Human beings feel a connection to each other and to all living things. In fact, we are hard-wired to be connected: when we see others suffering, portions of our brains respond empathically. We are compassionate and empathetic beings; when we witness the suffering of other people or animals, we act to do what we can to stop it.

A NUMBER OF years ago my friend Gayle, a woman I admired for her intelligence and good works, introduced me to The New York Women's Foundation, a charity that seeks to empower women to lift themselves out of poverty. I loved the idea of getting involved with a charity that helped women move forward both in terms of education and economics. It is my belief that women should be treated the equal of men and have the same opportunities. After researching The New York Women's Foundation and learning that they were an excellent charity, I decided to slowly get involved with them. I initially started by hosting and underwriting an annual luncheon for The New York Women's Foundation at Le Cirque in New York City for about 90 women. Today I am a very satisfied Board Member! I have given the luncheon for several years and will continue to do so for as long as possible. I also co-chair events and do volunteer fundraising for them. I am involved because I believe in their mission—The New York Women's Foundation supports and partners with organizations that work to improve the health, safety, and economic well-being of women and families in New York City. Each year these non-profits and grantee partners provide in-depth services to 57,000 women and girls and benefit about 400,000 people in the five boroughs of New York City! Through my involvement with The New York Women's Foundation, I know that I am helping not just the women of New York, but women around the globe. We serve as a model charity for many that seek to empower women! Below is a story of just one of the thousands of women helped by The New York Women's Foundation:

In 2011, Ela's dream came true when she won the green card lottery and migrated from Albania to America. Networking with friends, she quickly found work as a childcare provider for an Albanian family in New York City, making $10 per hour. However, she felt isolated; the family she worked for only spoke her native language in the home, providing very little opportunity for her to practice her English. That was when Ela learned about Hot Bread Kitchen's paid training program, a women's business that receives grants from The New York Women's Foundation. English fluency classes were also available, so Ela jumped at the opportunity and applied to the program.

As Ela focused on improving her English proficiency, she progressed to working the commercial ovens where her true talents shined. In April 2014, Ela was put on a fast-track towards graduation. Her training hours increased, and throughout the summer she improved both her English and baking skills. Her tenacity paid off in October 2014 when Ela graduated to a full-time position at Hot Bread Kitchen as the oven coordinator, earning $13.50 per hour with access to benefits.

Today, Ela is a lead baker at Hot Bread Kitchen, excelling in her supervisory role teaching the bakery trainees. She continues to improve her English, taking classes on her own time. Ela was quoted as saying, "I am thankful to Hot Bread Kitchen and The New York Women's Foundation for helping me learn how to speak English and to work at a job I love!"

We give because we know that suffering thrives on apathy. When we turn a blind eye to the suffering around us, our hopes for the future falter; the potential for the human race dims just a little further. In contrast, our decision to care, and our commitment to act *because* we care, brings light into the world. Giving means taking action when we see pain, suffering, and struggle.

We give because we are grateful. Each one of us is blessed in life. Giving is a profound way to say "thank you" and express gratitude for our blessings. We may give in honor of someone else, or carry on a tradition of giving instilled in us when we were young.

We give to demonstrate our love for others. Giving fuels more giving; once we start, the momentum of giving, even if it starts out small, can build into something with real impact. Giving is contagious; it can inspire others. There is no better way to express our gratitude for all we have been given in life than to give back.

CHARLES GREW UP humbly in New York City. He, his two siblings, and his parents lived in a two-room apartment. His parents slept on the pull-out sofa in the living room. Charles' parents instilled in him the need for a strong education and he worked diligently in school. Charles was able to get into an Ivy League college and then a top graduate school. Thanks to scholarship support, he received financing for most of his education. When Charles completed graduate school, he worked for a major Wall Street firm and, through hard work, became its youngest partner in history. He later married and had three children. As Charles grew to be more successful, he became actively involved in government and a number of charities that helped the most underserved. Charles lives a good life and has made it a priority to give of both his time and resources to help those in need.

MY PERSONAL EXPERIENCE OF GIVING

Each one of us writes our own story of giving.

Mine began while I was growing up on Long Island, New York, where I attended Catholic schools. My teachers and parents taught me the importance of caring for the less fortunate. It was then that I developed compassion for others and wanted to be of help. In high school, like many others, I would often try to assist a friend or neighbor in need. It was at this time that I decided to look for a career where I could be helpful to others. I later went on to earn a degree from Columbia University's College of Physicians and Surgeons, with a BS in Physical Therapy.

I began my work as a physical therapist at St. Luke's Hospital in New York City. While working at this inner city hospital, I saw tremendous human suffering.

Some people you meet, you never forget. At St. Luke's, I met a young woman with multiple sclerosis. She was married with four children. Her relationship with her husband was falling apart because of her condition and frequent hospitalizations. She spoke to me in confidence about how difficult her life was, and how desperately she worried about the well-being of her children. This was just one of many heart-wrenching cases I worked with.

The story of her struggle and that of many of the other patients stayed with me. I returned to Columbia and attended the Columbia Business School to earn my MBA in finance. During graduate school, I met my husband Martin. I had a short career on Wall Street and stopped working to be a full-time mother when my first daughter was born. While raising my two daughters, I began to help with fundraising at their schools. I was also active with a few charities. Once my daughters went off to college, I became fully engaged with philanthropic work.

Today, my charity work is more than a full-time job—it is my life. I live in New York City, a city where 30 percent of children live at or below the poverty level. I find it impossible to live here and not take action. I am committed to doing what I can, with the intention of helping to create positive change.

There are so many needs, and never enough resources. I have not limited my charitable interests to one or two causes; I have traveled to many places in the world, including many developing nations. A few years ago, when touring Cambodia, I spent time in an orphanage, toured a number of English learning schools, and was invited to visit many hut-like homes with no running water. Part of my time there was spent with the Cambodian Child's Dream Organization. This charity supplied water wells to groups of families, while also helping to fund the orphanage and the English-learning schools. Resources were extremely limited, and I was surrounded by poverty. I will never forget what I saw. When I left, I made it my business to supply the children at the two schools with new uniforms. I also helped to fund the water wells. While at the orphanage we were invited to purchase the artwork of the young children and I happily participated.

Today, I serve on several charity boards. Some require more work than others; however, they all need help. I truly am fortunate to be involved with them. I am most thankful for the opportunity to do this work and I love being a volunteer.

> We were put here on this earth to learn, to grow, and to give. We must make opportunities available to people so that they can improve their future.

OVERCOMING BLOCKS TO GIVING

The greatest gift is to be in a position to give back to society and understand that this is an important part of a fulfilling life.

However, giving can be a challenge for some. Giving may not come naturally, regardless of background. If the need to give was not instilled at a young age, it might be more difficult to understand the value and importance of philanthropy. After becoming a believer in a cause and gradually getting involved in a few nonprofits, every person can slowly begin to realize the value of giving.

No matter how aware we are of the benefits of giving, there are times when things seem to stand in the way of us taking action. We may feel our calendars are already too packed to accommodate more demands on our time. Or we may feel too exhausted to add any additional activities to our schedules. We may feel shy about working with people in need, or hesitant to reach outside of our comfort zone towards the others all around us who could use our help.

Sometimes we doubt that we have anything to contribute, and if our dollars are stretched, we may think to ourselves, "Now may not be the best time to give." It is understandable to be reluctant to dip into one's bank account when it seems that bills, big expenses, and everyday purchases already account for every dollar.

However, despite these obstacles, there is always something you can give. Take the time to examine your life to see where you might be helpful.

For example, Flo is a prominent radio broadcaster on shows syndicated across the nation. She also writes for a few media outlets. As the cost of living increased, she has found that her salary does not keep up with her monthly expenses. She struggles to pay her rent and make ends meet. Despite this, Flo finds ways to help a number of charities. She makes an effort to introduce others to causes she believes in. Flo also gets involved in selling tickets to charity benefits and bringing in auction prizes. In addition, she helps by promoting many causes she believes in on her radio show and through her media outlets. Flo understands that she can be helpful and does her part to contribute. Although Flo is not able to make financial contributions because of her own personal struggles, she is able to give in many other valuable ways. Flo is a practicing philanthropist.

THE VALUE OF GIVING

It is important to remember that giving is not a short-term, superficial experience. Giving is a force of life—and its source lies within us. Giving can come naturally to us. Our ability to give can adapt to our way of life. Giving can be of great value to us, in the most wonderful ways. Giving is self-fulfilling and makes us feel complete.

Giving provides perspective and allows us to contribute to the world. Each one of us can reap the uplifting benefits of giving. Giving provides relief from our day-to-day obligations and from the bombardment of information so ubiquitous in our modern culture. Because of the proliferation of smart phones, social media, and near-constant internet access, we can become exhausted by the constant demands on our time and attention. On top of all our regular responsibilities, the expectation that we be constantly reachable may make us feel like we are being stretched too thin.

Yet an opportunity to give back, even if only for a few hours a month, allows us to exit life's frantic pace for a while and step into what really matters: what we, as human beings, can do for those in need. Even a small period of time spent giving back can enrich our lives. When we give, we feel fulfilled knowing that we are not just thinking selfishly of ourselves, but rather about those who need our help.

WILLIAM ALLEN grew up in Harlem, in New York City, and was raised by his single mother. When William was young, he spent much of his free time at the Minisink Townhouse run by the NYC Mission Society. He participated in many of their after-school and summer programs. He credits NYC Mission Society for changing his life. Today, William Allen is Deputy Chief Clerk at the Board of Elections, a District Leader in Harlem, and a guest lecturer at several different colleges including the John Jay College of Criminal Justice. He is very grateful for all that NYC Mission Society has done to make his life so strong. William volunteers his time to NYC Mission Society. He is always encouraging alumni to become involved by sharing their experiences so that they can serve as role models and help to shape future generations with success stories. His story, along with others, reinforces the importance of this charity's work.

Giving energizes us and those around us. Sometimes it feels like there are not enough hours in the day. How could we possibly find the energy to volunteer, when we barely have enough time for ourselves, families, and friends?

There is nothing more gratifying than the feeling of helping someone else out. It elevates us out of our own concerns and takes us to a place where we feel a profound connection to the value of life. Experiencing the power of what it means to give back can sustain us and enliven us. If we have the time or financial resources to give back, taking action is incredibly rewarding and can be a great learning experience. Of course, it's important not to push ourselves over the limits of what we can do. For those times in life when it is harder to give, such as when we are busy raising a family, we can still teach the value of giving to our children, and do our part in small ways.

3

BUILDING A LIFE AROUND GIVING

"How wonderful that no one need wait a single moment to improve the world."

—ANNE FRANK

A S A PHILANTHROPIST, you write your own *story of giving* that unfolds over a lifetime. This story of giving can adapt as your own personal life circumstances change and evolve.

Philanthropy benefits others around us and expands our life experiences. Any and all efforts we make to look past our own lives, to meet the struggles that other people face head-on, and to do what we can to make the world a better place broadens our perspectives and gives us a new appreciation for the power we have to change things.

Even if, at the present moment, your gift of time or financial resources must be small, you can always build in more giving as the years go by. *Those in need will always benefit from your contribution.*

WHO: PHILANTHROPY BEGINS WITH YOU

Philanthropy begins with you.

You can make the decision to help manifest positive change.

You can adopt a profound shift in perspective: to start thinking in terms of what you can offer to aid those in need around you.

You can decide to take action on behalf of those who need help.

But it isn't only about you. Your philanthropic efforts can have a profound effect on others, too. When you give, you not only help those individuals facing hardship—you also inspire those around you. People *can* be taught to give. By your actions, you set a powerful example for the people close to you. Your acts of giving can multiply through the people you know. You can welcome others into giving with you. Bringing partners, children (if they are the right age), coworkers, and friends when you volunteer allows you to spend time with each other and help those in need at the same time.

Volunteering with coworkers can be especially enriching; it is an opportunity to get out of the office and see another side to your colleagues. You may even discover skills that can be put to work back in the office environment.

WHEN TO GIVE: GIVING OVER A LIFETIME

For all of us, the best time to give is *whenever we can*.

When life gets complicated, giving can adapt to life's challenges and demands. The only thing that is certain in life is change. It is to be expected that the nature and extent of our personal giving might change if and when our life's circumstances change. By being aware of our limitations and working with what we *can* do, it is possible to give at all ages and stages of life.

For example, when you are busy raising a family and working, sharing your time and knowledge by volunteering may be too much for your packed schedule. Under these circumstances, making donations may be a better choice.

At other times, we may have the available time to give but not the financial resources. For those who are young and just starting out in their careers, extra income may be hard to come by, but free time and extra energy may mean it makes sense to volunteer at the end of the workday or on a weekend, to lend time to a cause that's important.

GIVING AT A YOUNG AGE

Children must be educated about the importance of giving at a young age. Children must learn the importance of philanthropy from teachers, parents, religious institutions, and the community. Parents must teach their children the value of helping those in need. Parents can set a good example by their involvement with philanthropy and then by teaching their children. Schools should make courses on giving and philanthropy part of their required curriculum. Courses on giving that include community service are now being taught in some schools, but these courses need to be in every school and college.

The importance of aiding those in need is often taught or preached as a part of religious instruction in churches, synagogues, and mosques. Communities often organize activities that promote their young citizens to participate in giving back.

> The more children are exposed to philanthropy, the more they will be inclined to participate. Children can also learn the value of philanthropy by *seeing it in action*.

Encouraging your children to give back can be a fulfilling experience that draws you together. It can be empowering for them to choose which cause they might want to get involved in. Children love to be with their peers, so including your child's friends in volunteer work can make the act of giving far more appealing. Is your child moved by the struggle of animals? Does your child want to do his or her part to stop a species from becoming endangered or extinct? A parent can help find a charity that addresses issues that are of interest to the child. Maybe a child loves playing at a local park. If so, participating in a local child-friendly fundraiser for the park could be a fun way to engage them in giving.

The more children learn to give as they grow, the more likely it is that they will have a deep-rooted understanding of the benefits of giving. Later, they can enter the world with a comprehension of how important it is for them to reach past themselves and their own wants, desires, and needs to embrace helping other people. Enabling children to get involved in philanthropy encourages them to see their place in society. It empowers them as individuals to make positive change in the world.

GIVING IN THE YOUNG ADULT AND MIDDLE YEARS

Many young adults become involved with philanthropy by getting involved with junior groups of favorite charities. Often a young person might get involved for a variety of reasons. He or she might be drawn to the mission of a charity as well as the social aspects of joining a young junior group.

RYAN WAS A young executive working at an advertising firm just outside of New York City. Although he lived in the city, he found that his work made it difficult for him to meet young people. Ryan also felt the need to add meaning to his life by getting involved with a worthwhile cause. He had heard about the charity galas hosted by New Yorkers for Children, which attracted a group of young professionals. Not only did he have a few friends who attended their galas, but he also liked the fact that the charity helped children in the foster care system. Through his involvement with New Yorkers for Children, Ryan met and started to date Beth. Together, they went to social events hosted by the charity. They enjoyed all the friends they met, but more importantly, they also felt like they were doing something to benefit children in need. Even though Ryan did not have much time to give, he felt more fulfilled in his personal life because of New Yorkers for Children. Ryan has promised himself that, when he has more time, he will become more involved with the charity.

Brooke and Cole founded the junior group of the New York City Mission Society shortly after serving on the charity's Bicentennial Gala's Associates Committee in 2012. "We started it because we wanted to engage the next generation of philanthropists in New York City, create buzz and awareness, fundraise, and volunteer," says Cole, whose family has been supportive of the Mission Society for generations. The Junior Society organizes small fundraising cocktail parties and events, as well as a holiday toy drive which garners hundreds of toys for underserved children. "We saw an organization that we both truly believe in, and want to give our peers an opportunity to engage and give back," says Brooke.

Young married couples with children often get involved with charities. It is a way for families to connect with one another and to feel they are doing something useful for society outside of their own personal lives. Many charities have divisions that cater to young families. Family charity fundraising activities such as sports events, barbecues, and entertainment nights all add interest to life and help to engage young families in philanthropy!

GIVING DURING RETIREMENT

During retirement, the demands of work are lifted and most people find that they have more spare time than ever before. Retirees can give back in incredible ways. Often, retirees have a wealth of knowledge and greater available savings to give to nonprofit organizations. A life's worth of insight and lessons learned— including lessons from the frontlines of running a company, managing a household, and leading successful careers—can change other peoples' lives. Usually, retirees can devote more time and resources to charities than younger working people might be able to.

THE POWER OF FAMILIES THAT GIVE BACK

A philanthropic family can be an amazing resource. Some philanthropic families are famous because of their wealth. By the time of his death in 1937, John D. Rockefeller had donated $540 million over the course of nearly 80 years. Since then, the Rockefeller name has been behind a legacy of philanthropic giving, from founding universities, museums, and national parks, as well as foundations that provide thousands of dollars in grant funding each year.

Today, famous philanthropic families include Bill Gates and his wife Melinda (over $34.5 billion in grants since inception); Michael Bloomberg (over $3 billion); the Waltons (of Wal-Mart; $325 million in 2013 alone); and Ted Turner and his family (the Turner Foundation, over $350 million since 1990), to name a few.

But philanthropic families are not just wealthy families. Any family that makes an effort to give back is a philanthropic family. If every family in America made giving a part of how they spend their family time and money, and passed along the value of giving to their children, the amount of good we could do is simply staggering. If each member of a four-person family chose to give over a lifetime and gave consistently over five decades, their combined efforts would provide the equivalent of roughly 200 years' worth of giving back!

WHAT TO GIVE

Whether you make a donation or share your time, the number one rule is to *give what you are comfortable giving*. Take the time to really think about what you are realistically able to give, whether it is money and/or time. Carefully consider what is realistic for you and your own resources.

FINANCIAL CONTRIBUTIONS

If you do decide to make a monetary gift, start by identifying what is possible within your budget.

Be realistic about what you can afford; no one has limitless resources. Do not feel compelled to give more than you are comfortable with. Remember, every gift is meaningful, even if it is small. It is far better to start out with a small gift that fits your budget than to give more than you can handle and end up feeling financially strained. You can always give more at a later date, when larger donations become more manageable for you.

Some people find it helpful to budget their giving throughout the year. Others choose an amount based on a percentage of income (this works best for those whose incomes are fairly stable).

If your life recently changed due to marriage, a new partner, expanding your family, or a shift in your career trajectory, your expenses may have become more complicated; consider volunteering your time or giving back in other ways until your finances stabilize.

VOLUNTEERING YOUR TIME OR SHARING YOUR KNOWLEDGE OR EXPERTISE

Your unique energies, talents, and abilities can benefit many. When it comes to volunteering your time, your help can be very meaningful, even if you do not have many hours to spare.

Work *with* your schedule, instead of against it. First, take your personal responsibilities into account as you consider your availability. Family time and work obligations take precedence. From there, take a look at the time you have free. Ask yourself how you spend that free time. Be honest; do you feel like you are wasting your free time?

Time is our most valuable asset! How we spend our time is how we spend our lives. Although it may be hard to motivate ourselves to get out of the house on the weekends or spend a little time once a week volunteering after work, the experience is well worth the effort: helping others brings rewards that are enriching. Often volunteer work can be the most fulfilling way to spend leisure time.

MICHAEL FOUND that he had excess spare time once his 9 to 5 job ended. He felt that his Wall Street job did not provide enough meaning to his life. In addition, he had recently ended a relationship and wanted to fill his time away from work. Michael decided to volunteer at a local food pantry on the weekends. He found the volunteer work to be rewarding, and it also helped to get his mind off his recent split with his girlfriend. He loved working with those who came into the soup kitchen for a hot meal. The gratitude they showed towards him and the other volunteers gave more meaning to his life. He felt appreciated and believed he was helping to make a difference. In addition, he met other young volunteers who he discovered had similar priorities and found that he truly enjoyed their company.

Whatever time you have available is valuable, and even minimal involvement is still meaningful. It is perfectly fine to get started slowly, and increase your commitment over time. If you're a parent (depending on the age of your children), you should also consider bringing your family into your charitable giving (see page 203). Even donating a few hours every few months will help you keep up the habit of volunteering your time.

WHERE TO GIVE

Finding a charity that is of particular interest to you can be overwhelming at first. There are so many worthy causes in the world and so many people that need help.

Thankfully, there are specific strategies and steps you can take to simplify the process. See Chapter 4 for guidelines on choosing a charity. Chapter 4 will also examine steps you should consider if you are interested in joining the board of a charity.

VOLUNTEERING WITH A CHARITY

Volunteers play a vital role in the life of a charity. For many charities, there is simply too much work to rely only on their paid staff. This is where volunteers come in. It is nearly impossible to measure the positive value that volunteers can contribute; the impact of volunteers goes way beyond simply providing an hourly service for which charities would otherwise have to pay employees. Volunteers who step in to help a charity end up boosting the charity's mission, helping people in need, and often provide a wealth of energy, experience, and knowledge in addition to the gift of their time.

When you sign on to help out a charity, you could take on any number of roles, from answering phones, helping to send out mail, fundraising, selling tickets, reading with or tutoring children, or counseling those in need. Carefully consider not only what skills you have, but what talents and abilities you would most enjoy using. Most charities should be willing to try and place you in a role based on what your strengths are; this will benefit them as well. If you have a physical impairment or other specific issue, be sure to share it with the charity so that they can do their best to accommodate you.

Each charity will have different volunteer needs. After you make a list of your skills and abilities, you will have to reach out to the charity to determine if what you have to offer matches up with their volunteer requests. Don't be surprised if you are asked to come in for an interview; the process is as much about helping you figure out where you best fit in as it is for the charity itself.

Take some time to do a brief self-assessment to identify your personal goals and strengths. Ask yourself:

- How much time can I realistically give in a week, a month, or a year?

- When am I available to volunteer, and during what hours of the day?

- What special talents, skills, or knowledge do I possess that I can offer to help this charity reach their goals? (Consult the charity's mission statement online, or, if you need clarification on their mission, give them a call and ask.)

- What tasks or duties am I unwilling, or unable, to do?

Also ask yourself what you hope to *gain* out of the experience. Feeling gratified and enthused by what you are doing will ultimately fuel your giving over the long-term, and benefit both the charity and its recipients further.

Again, time and available resources play a role in the amount of involvement one can have in charitable causes. A young person who is going to school and working part-time or full-time will have less time to devote to charity.

Likewise, young mothers and fathers will also have more limited time than a retiree. You can still do charity work and give resources; your involvement may just be more limited. Whatever you can give is still valuable, and will be appreciated by any charity you end up working with.

GETTING INVOLVED IN YOUR COMMUNITY

Giving in your community can be rewarding. The efforts of your work can be seen right in front of you. There are numerous ways to give back to the community, and individuals of all ages can participate. A school-age child can be involved in a charitable event at church or school. Young working people can get involved with the many junior divisions that exist for charity groups, and can help mentor young people by being a big brother or big sister. Busy mothers and fathers can try to find a little time to volunteer at their children's schools, or become involved with charity groups aimed at young families.

NEW YORK CITY
MISSION SOCIETY

In 2012, I had just finished chairing the Southampton Animal Shelter Gala. It was mid-August, and I was back in New York City. I had recently been asked to co-chair the 200th Anniversary Gala of the New York City Mission Society, which was to take place on 12/12/12. NYC Mission Society is an anti-poverty charity that works with the most underserved children in New York City. The Minisink Townhouse, where many of their programs take place, is located in Harlem, at 142nd Street and Lenox Avenue.

Although I had heard wonderful things about the work of NYC Mission Society, I knew that before I said yes to serving as Chair for their Bicentennial Gala, it would be important to see their programs in action. I also knew that I would need to do research on their programs and the charity itself. After doing a fair amount of research on NYC Mission and learning that they were a well-run charity, I decided it would be best to go on a site visit of their programs before agreeing. So on a very hot August afternoon, I toured the Minisink Townhouse. There I saw a type of city "summer camp" in progress. Although there was no pool or swimming program, the children were engaged in soccer and a variety of classes, including tap-dancing, music, geography, and classes on long- and short-term goals. Young student ambassadors provided a guided tour of all the summer activities in progress. Children ages 6 to 18 were engaged in the program and seemed very happy. The children were polite and respectful.

These were children who might otherwise be hanging out on street corners with nothing to do. The children all lived at or below the poverty level. I left feeling very moved by what I had seen and knew that I wanted to become involved with NYC Mission Society. It was not a question of *if* I was going to get involved; rather, it was simply that I *must* become involved.

And that was how I got started with NYC Mission Society. I went on to co-chair the New York City Mission Society's 200th Anniversary Gala in 2012. One year later, they asked if they could honor me with the Dina Merrill Award for Public Service at their upcoming gala. As an honoree I knew that I would be expected to help raise funds, make a financial gift, and introduce them to new people. They were looking for two more honorees, so I introduced them to Val, a senior partner of a major Wall Street firm who was active with many charities, and suggested that they make him an honoree. He accepted!

I then suggested that they honor another financier, Steve, who was involved in starting the first charter school in New York. Steve accepted, but decided that he wanted to be honored in a group, along with the other founders of the charter school. The event was a success, and in late 2014 I joined their board. Serving on any board can be a lot of work, but it is very rewarding. I know that by serving on the board on New York City Mission Society, I am involved with helping to change the lives of many of New York City's children who are most in need.

THE BENEFITS OF WHAT YOU HAVE TO OFFER

Ask yourself:

What can I do to help alleviate suffering?

How can I be useful?

All the benefit that you can bring to others waits on your decision. Will you engage in philanthropy? The longer you wait to share what you can offer, the longer others in need struggle without the benefit of your knowledge and help. Your journey as a philanthropist begins when you decide that you want to take action.

4

HOW TO CHOOSE
A CHARITY

"*The Golden Rule...points us in a clear direction. Let us treat others with the same passion and compassion with which we want to be treated. Let us seek for others the same possibilities which we seek for ourselves.*"

—POPE FRANCIS TO US
CONGRESS, 2015

T O GIVE HOPE to others through charity is to do God's work on earth. That being said, how do you make up your mind about what charity to support? The first step is to find a cause that is of interest to you and that you are passionate about. If you are going to give financially, or give the gift of time, you will want to believe in the cause! Contributing to a cause that is close to your heart lays the groundwork for a fulfilling experience.

That being said, choosing a charity is not just about finding one that personally interests you; it also requires that you do research. You will want to make sure that you are getting involved with a well-run charity. Look at all the facts before deciding on a charity—in terms of both its programs and finances. While it takes some research to educate yourself about an organization, by doing so you can feel assured that you are making a good decision, and that you will be making the best use of your gifts of time and money.

This chapter will help you determine your interests. Then it will take you through the steps you will need to follow in order to research a charity. Finally, this chapter will explore what is expected of most charities when they look for board members. All of this will help you determine where you might want to get involved, and how involved you might like to become.

SOUTHAMPTON HOSPITAL GALA

A number of years ago, I was asked to chair the Southampton Hospital Gala. Prior to then, I had served both as an auction chair and vice chair of the Hospital's Gala. Knowing that the job of Chairwoman—the sole Chairwoman responsible for one of the very largest events in the Hamptons—would be a great deal of work, I had to think about the decision carefully. Not only would it require that I be very involved in organizing a party for close to 1,000 people, but it would require reaching out to many people in the community and asking them to volunteer their time or give donations which ranged from small amounts to up to $100,000 for the event. As Chairwoman, I would also be required to bring in corporate sponsorship. It would be an honor to accept the responsibility, but I had to think carefully about whether I had the time, and if I could do a good job.

After doing research on the Southampton Hospital and becoming convinced that the Hospital was well managed, I accepted the position of Chairwoman. Next, I set aside large pockets of my time to devote to this responsibility. I made chairing this event a priority. Volunteer fundraising is both difficult and rewarding. I was told I did a very good job and was asked to chair again the next year, and then a third time. The total amount raised in those three years from the parties was $5.4 million!

Ultimately, the reason why I said yes to chairing this event so many times was because I believe that health care in all communities is one of the most important causes to support. The Southampton Hospital services thousands of people who cannot afford healthcare. Without good health care, a community cannot flourish. I do not think there is a person on this earth who would dispute the importance of quality health care. So, although I had to work very hard, I did so gladly, because of my passion for the cause.

A PASSION AND A CAUSE

The first thing you will need to do is to find a cause that is of interest to you. Often, people become passionate about a cause and this passion fuels an interest to become involved. Start by asking the question, "What causes are most important to me?"

For example, if you are interested in improving education for underserved children in your community, look for a charity that does this. Or, if you love art and would like to see your local museum grow, make it your goal to get involved with the museum.

If you have trouble pinpointing your cause of choice, look to your own life for guidance. Here are some suggested approaches:

Decide based on what brings you joy. Look to what you find enriching in your own life. If you enjoy walks through the local park then volunteering to work in a public garden or donating funds to help build and maintain a park could be a rewarding way for you to get involved in philanthropy. If visiting a museum is something you regularly enjoy, working with a cultural institution could be fulfilling. You can share your joy and appreciation with others in your community and around the world.

Choose based on where you want to see changes. When you read or watch the news, what do you wish could be different? Are there particular issues or causes that you feel strongly about? Consider how and where you would like to see change. Then, tap into your power of giving to take action and do your part.

Look to help others around you. Look to honor the memory of a loved one. Our lives are enriched by those around us. This understanding can be the basis for meaningful giving. Does a loved one suffer from a disease and do you want to help a non-profit organization help find a cure for this disease? Often, we are compelled to get involved with a charity that addresses a problem that someone we love is suffering from. For example, Jennifer's husband Tom suffered from bi-polar disorder. Jennifer made it her business to get involved with a major hospital in Boston that funded research addressing this disorder. She wanted to help her husband and others who suffered, so she decided she would donate funding to their efforts to find better ways to treat those suffering with bi-polar disorder. Jennifer felt great relief by doing this and her husband was pleased with all she did to try to be of help.

Do you feel compelled to help in memory of someone who was close to you? You can choose to honor a loved one by volunteering or giving in their memory. If someone you love has survived an illness or other hardship and benefited from the support of a foundation or organization, you may feel inspired to give your time as a show of gratitude and appreciation on their behalf. For example, Amanda's mother, Christine, had struggled with breast cancer for the last several years of her life. Although Christine had not participated in any charities involved in breast cancer research, Amanda decided to get involved with the local branch of a national charity allied with finding a cure. Amanda did this to honor her mother's memory; she did not want others to suffer as her mother had during the course of her last years. By getting involved with this charity, Amanda believed that her mother would be proud of her and her good work. Amanda found comfort in honoring her mother in this way. She also felt strongly about being involved in a charity that wanted to help others who suffer with breast cancer.

Reflect on what has meant the most to you in the course of your life. As we grow, each one of us is shaped by our experiences, and the mentors and great minds that have guided us along our way. If you look back on the experiences that played the greatest role in shaping your character, you will most likely be inspired to give back. If your education set you on the path to a meaningful life, consider giving back to your high school or college alumni organization. By doing so, you can help the institution or organization continue their work for the next generation. Consider what you are grateful for, and ask yourself how you can share the same opportunities you were given with others.

Remember, there is no reason to limit yourself to one choice; you can work with or donate to a number of organizations. Just be realistic about what you can do based on your free time and available financial resources.

THE HATHERLEIGH FOUNDATION

The Hatherleigh Foundation works to advance causes in five primary areas: health, education, career opportunity, world peace, and the environment. The Hatherleigh Foundation builds its work on the tenant that innovation and giving are inexorably linked, and that by providing support for creativity and forward-thinking initiatives, the giving that results will lead to real change. The Hatherleigh Foundation focuses on several key principles, including efforts to harness the power of the people and work that fosters generosity in others today, not tomorrow. The Hatherleigh Foundation advances the work of individuals and start-ups that support the principles of wellness and healthful living, consistent practice of peace, individual productivity and job opportunities, and an earth-consciousness that guards the future of the planet and the animals that inhabit it.

CATEGORIES OF CHARITIES AND CAUSES

When it comes to choosing a charity and a cause, the choices—in the United States and around the world—are numerous. To simplify the categorization process, the website Charity Navigator (www.charitynavigator.org) groups charities into 11 different *categories*, with each category divided into more narrowly defined *causes*.

BELOW IS THE list of 11 categories, with examples of some causes within each category to help you narrow down your cause of choice:

1. Animal Charities *such as animal rights; wildlife conservation; zoos and aquariums*

2. Arts, Culture & Humanities *such as libraries, historical societies and landmark preservation; museums; performing arts; public broadcasting*

3. Community Development *such as fundraising; community organizations; housing and neighborhood development*

4. Education *such as universities, colleges, and graduate schools; elementary schools; other educational programs and services*, as well as job training

5. Environment *such as environmental protection and conservation; parks, nature centers, and gardens*

6. Health *such as those treating disorders and diseases; patient and family support; treatment and prevention; medical research*

7. Human and Civil Rights *such as advocacy and education*

8. Human Services *such as children and family services; youth shelter and crisis services; food banks and food pantries; multi-purpose services, homeless services, and social services*

9. International *such as development and relief; peace and security; single country support*

10. Research and Public Policy *such as non-medical science and technology research; social and public policy*

11. Religion *such as religious activities; media and broadcasting*

CHOOSING A CHARITY: DOING THE RESEARCH

While choosing a charity is an exciting venture, it can also be a challenge. Most charities are run well, but it is your responsibility to decide wisely and to practice intelligent giving. Here are just a few suggestions that will be very helpful to you and that should guide your research.

Once you have targeted a charity that interests you, try to find out all you can about how its operations are run. In order to do this, you will need to do some research. There are a few charity websites that can be very helpful with research. Two recommended websites are Charity Navigator (www.charitynavigator.org) and GuideStar (www.guidestar.org). Both rate various charities on performance and will help you access information on how well a charity is performing its work. Please note that not all charities are rated on these two websites. In general, the smaller the charity, the more likely it will not be rated by either group.

A NONPROFIT ORGANIZATION is required to file a 990 form with the IRS each year to report their income and expenses. It is similar to the 1040 form that individuals are required to file. The 990 form allows the IRS and the public to evaluate nonprofits and how they operate. In recent years, the 990 form has been revised to collect more information such as disclosure of potential conflicts of interest, and other details having to do with financial accountability and avoidance of fraud.

As of 2010, the GuideStar database contained over 5 million IRS 990 forms submitted by nearly two million organizations. Before choosing a charity, it is a good idea to look at the organization's 990 form. A good charity will give you access to their audited financial statements. If you do not know how to interpret a 990 form, ask someone with a strong business background to review it for you. It should be noted that countless charitable organizations, especially smaller grassroots organizations, do not run at a surplus/profit. Many nonprofits rely on philanthropic dollars to break even or have a very small profit. For example, small hospitals can operate for years and not break even, or they run on a surplus from operational income and rely upon philanthropic resources to break even or earn a surplus.

During the course of your research you will need to look for answers to the following questions.

Are the charity's operating expenses low, relative to their revenues? You will want to be involved with a charity that is well run and that has low operating expenses. Well run charities should have annual operating expenses which are *20 percent or less of their revenue*. In general, the lower the operating expenses, the better. A charity should make this information available to you upon request.

Does the charity operate at a surplus or deficit? The nonprofit you get involved with should operate with a surplus each year.

How much of the charity's revenue is actually going towards its programs? One of the major reasons why you will choose a charity is because of the work of its programs. An important fact for you to know is how much of a charity's revenue is going towards the programs they run. In general, the higher the percentage going towards program operations the better. You should be able to obtain this information from a financial officer of the charity.

THE ROBIN HOOD FOUNDATION

In 1988, the Robin Hood Foundation was founded by Paul Tudor Jones. This Foundation works to alleviate poverty and provide disaster assistance in New York City and surrounding areas. Like Robin Hood, known for bestowing wealth to the poor, the Robin Hood Foundation distributes funds across several nonprofits in New York City and its environs. To date, they have worked with over 200 different organizations, providing funding to help numerous organizations continue their direct outreach to those in need. With a disciplined system in place to evaluate eligible organizations, the Foundation gives to those that have the most impact. Over $126 million went to fight poverty in New York City in 2013 alone, in addition to $56 million to help those recovering from Hurricane Sandy. The Foundation is incredibly successful at raising funds; in May of 2015 their gala raised over $101 million for charity! The Robin Hood Foundation prides itself that 100% of every donation they accept goes directly to fighting poverty.

Does the charity have strong leadership? Good leadership is vitally important to all charities. Do the leaders have good reputations? Are the leaders committed to the cause? Are they in it for the long run? If you are uncertain how to determine this, then ask others in the same field who might know the leaders of the given charity. You can also look up a leader's background online.

Are they working to fulfill their mission statement? Take the time to learn about the charity's mission statement and then do the research to find out if they are working to achieve their goals. This may also entail looking at the financial statements to see that they are using their funds wisely to realize their mission. If you do not know how to read the financial statements, ask someone with a business background to help you with your evaluation.

Do you believe that the charity has good programs? Read all you can about the work of the charity's programs. Don't be afraid to ask questions. Request to go on a site visit. Most charities will welcome the opportunity to take interested individuals on a site visit.

Does the charity have a good reputation? Find out about the charity's reputation. If the charity has historically been plagued with problems, you may wish to think carefully before getting involved.

Can you easily be involved with the nonprofit? Does the charity have a local chapter? If a charity is based in Washington D.C. and you live in Seattle, you may find it very difficult to become involved. Ask yourself if you can realistically become involved long distance. Find out if the charity has a local chapter. If there is no local chapter, you might want to pass and find a similar charity that is located nearby.

I F YOU are planning on volunteering and you have limited time during the week, it may be possible to choose a place to volunteer based on location; for example, if you know you want to work with children in an after-school program, and several schools in your area offer applicable programs, you may want to narrow down your options based on what is easier for your commute.

Does the charity treat its volunteers well?
You as a volunteer will want to be treated with dignity and respect. Likewise, you will want to treat those involved with the charity the same way—with dignity and respect.

Ask yourself: Do you think you can add value to the charity? Do you think that your skills are of value to a particular charity? There are charities that have far too many volunteers and not enough work for all of them. If this is the case, it may make sense to look for a charity where your time and skills are valued and needed. One way to determine this is by reaching out to a charity and then observing their reaction to you. If there isn't much of a response, they may be telling you something. If you think another good charity might value your time and resources more, then you should probably look to that charity and think about getting involved with them.

Are you comfortable with the people involved with the charity? Look for a group where you think you fit in. Your comfort level with the people you work with is very important. Make sure that the people you're working with respect you and are courteous. It is important to feel like you belong and are an integral part of the group. You will want to be part of the team. If you don't feel comfortable and you do not like the way you are being treated, then it is probably a good indication you should look for another charity.

Does the charity do its job? One way of determining this is to talk to people who are involved with the charity. Take the time to read articles by those who have done an in-depth analysis. Review the charity's website, read all you can about their work, and then review the opinions of people who are involved with and know of the charity. Ask those whose opinion you respect and who you think might be knowledgeable and unbiased about the charity.

Do you think the charity has a strong board?
The Board Members of a charity tell a great deal about a nonprofit. In general, a well run charity has a strong board.

SERVING ON A BOARD: EXPECTATIONS AND REQUIREMENTS

Before you contemplate serving on a board, you should find out exactly what your responsibilities will be as a board member. Do not move forward unless you believe the charity is well run and feel certain that you would feel proud to be associated with that group, the work that they do, and the way in which they handle their resources. It would be wise to visit some of their programs to see their work in action. You may also wish to speak to others about the charity's reputation and work.

Remember that you can be very involved in a charity and not serve on their board. Many people become involved with a charity as a volunteer, without ever joining a board. Don't underestimate your value as a non-board member. Oftentimes, there may be volunteers who work harder and offer more than certain board members. Most volunteers serve a very important role in the success of a charity; you do not have to be on the board to be of great value.

Serving on a board can be a big commitment. Most boards will expect you to work on outreach. If this is the case, make sure you are comfortable working on outreach and making connections with sponsors and potential donors.

Most nonprofit boards have specific expectations required of their board members. There are exceptions, such as when a board might want an individual for his or her life experience, government involvement, or because of the value that his or her name can bring to them. In most cases, boards looks for members who can add to their mission and purpose in specific ways.

Before you join a charity board, have a serious discussion with that group's board president to find out exactly what is expected of you as a board member. Again, not all boards have specific requirements, but most do, and you will need to know what they are before you agree to join.

The following are some of the general hopes and expectations of a charity when they look for new board members. In general, most charities look for board members who are interested in promoting their objectives and who are compatible together. Not all boards will require all of the factors listed below; they may require only a few. These points should help determine whether joining a board is something you might want to pursue.

Passion for the cause. Boards look for members who are passionate about the charity's mission. With passion for a cause comes the desire to do more for the charity.

Financial donations. It is rare that board members are *not* asked to give personally. Before you agree to join a board, make sure you know what is financially expected of you. Do not be afraid to ask what is expected; and don't join the board if you cannot give, or do not want to give, at the expected level.

Fundraising expectations. Often, board members are expected to bring in contributions from corporations, foundations, and/or individuals. Try to find out the dollar amount that the board might expect you to raise. Often, the amount is not specifically defined, but you should always seek this information before you join.

Experience, knowledge, and ideas. Individuals are asked to join a board because they possess helpful knowledge, experience, and ideas. Individuals who have served on a number of charity boards can bring several helpful ideas they have learned elsewhere. When it comes to successfully serving on a board, knowledge is paramount and highly valued.

Personal contacts. An individual who can connect a charity to possible donors and new potential board members can be a key asset to a board. This person may not ask directly for funds, but can connect a development officer or the head of the charity to various groups and individuals that can donate.

A good business or personal reputation. Individuals with good reputations can bring others to a charity based on their participation alone. Boards are very cognizant of this, and look for board members with good reputations. Strong powerful names are highly valued by boards.

Government representation. A board may want to have a government official as a member. Government officials generally do not vote on board matters and are considered ex-officio. A number of charities work directly with governments (city, state, or national) to achieve their goals.

Ability to get along with other board members and the team of workers at a charity. Key to adding new members to a board is finding individuals who are positive and who get along with the other board members. A troublemaker or someone who looks to cause problems is a red flag to any board. No board wants a board member who creates trouble, gossips, or tries to destroy the morale of the others.

MOST BOARDS require that their board members sign a conflict of interest statement, which guarantees that they do not do any business with the charity and that they do not have a controlling interest in any business that does business with the charity.

5

HOW TO TREAT VOLUNTEERS, PAID EMPLOYEES, THOSE SERVICED BY A CHARITY, AND DONORS

"Do unto others as you would have done unto you."

—MATTHEW 7:12

ONE OF THE best aspects of volunteering with a charity is being able to work alongside dedicated men and women who are just as passionate about your chosen cause as you are! Joining an organization as a volunteer means becoming part of an important team, one where everyone works together for a common cause and the greater good. It is through this cooperative effort, joining talent and ideas together with collective energy and enthusiasm, that charities are able to achieve incredible results and meaningful change.

HOW TO BE A GOOD VOLUNTEER

As a team member, politeness and respect is a two-way street: you, as a volunteer, must be treated well. You, as a volunteer, must treat *others* well, too. Good manners, respect for other volunteers and members of the organization, and a positive attitude are important qualities in a good volunteer. It also means being respectful to all those you come into contact with. This obviously includes all those served by a charity.

Respectful communication among all those involved or served by a charity is imperative. This is true regardless of whether someone is a volunteer or a paid employee. Being a part of a charity means navigating various relationships, including those with employees, other volunteers, as well as donors, potential donors, and those served by the charity.

> Positive relationship-building is vital to the success of a charity, and so all communication must be founded on the principles of kindness, dignity, and respect.

Follow the guidelines below to ensure that work is pleasant for everyone where you volunteer and that things get done efficiently:

Practice good manners in person, over the phone, and via e-mail. Remember that as a volunteer you are representing your organization. Make sure your communication is in line with their values and policy.

Be respectful to others. You represent yourself as a volunteer. It is critically important to show others respect by being on time, not cancelling your scheduled volunteer time slot, and coming through on any promises of offers that you make. All of this demonstrates your commitment to helping others.

Be positive. As a volunteer, you have the opportunity to be a new source of energy and enthusiasm for the charity. An upbeat, can-do attitude will be appreciated by everyone. Show respect to those you meet: potential donors, friends of the charity, those who you work with, and those you serve.

Keep in mind that taking your work seriously does not mean you cannot enjoy it, too! Leave your personal dilemmas at the door. Volunteering is a great opportunity to be engaged in activities that will help others. The work should be gratifying. It is an opportunity to take a break from your own personal concerns.

VOLUNTEERING IN SOMEONE ELSE'S WORKPLACE

If you are spending considerable time working alongside employees of the charity, keep in mind that you are volunteering at someone else's workplace.

Like any office, there is a specific culture and set of rules in place. Everyone is there to support the same cause. The rules of conduct for you are the same as they are for someone who works full- or part-time as a paid employee of the organization.

Strive to be helpful. Initially, try not to make big changes to the way things are done. Do not presume to know how to do things better than others. If you have a suggestion, offer your opinion politely. Remember, your input can be valuable;

your opinion counts. That being said, do not take it personally if all of your suggestions are not utilized. You are part of a team and will need to be a good team player.

TREATING VOLUNTEERS WELL

Volunteers are unpaid workers who provide valuable resources. A volunteer who does not feel that he/she is being treated well or being appreciated can easily get up and walk away from a charity.

Be sure that you treat your fellow volunteers with respect—and that you are working in an environment that is respectful. Charities that become very cliquey and gossipy often lose the very best volunteers *and* major donors. Both paid workers and volunteers need to think in terms of "inclusion" rather than "exclusion." The team approach is often the best approach, and a good team leader will know that working together as a group is most effective for everyone and leads to the greatest amount of success for the charity.

TREATMENT OF PAID EMPLOYEES

All employees should be treated with dignity and respect. Paid employees are generally hired because of their expertise and knowledge. They are there to add value to the work of the charity and to get a job done. They generally work very hard. If you are a volunteer, you must be respectful to them. Also remember, paid employees need to be thanked just like anyone else.

TREATMENT OF THOSE SERVICED BY A CHARITY

It goes without saying that those serviced by a charity must be treated with kindness, dignity, and respect. As a volunteer, you will need to be very conscious of this. You represent the charity and must treat those who receive the services of the charity with great care. Always be polite, respectful, and helpful.

TREATMENT OF DONORS

All potential donors and donors must be treated with kindness and respect. Too often, those involved with a charity—either employees or volunteers—may underestimate the potential of both corporate and individual donors. Sometimes, an individual supporter can go on for years attending an event and act only moderately interested in the cause. Make certain to pay attention to the person who attends an event year after year. Never underestimate the potential of someone like this. Sometimes, long-term supporters (those who give many small gifts over time) will give a large sum to a charity later or decide to become very involved with the charity at some point in the future. Or, they may even leave a gift for the charity in their will. If someone is there all the time to show his or her support, make sure you show your appreciation.

Charities may review an individual's giving history and assume that this is all the individual will ever donate. As a result, they avoid spending time treating that person well and focus instead on other donors. Many times, I have seen charity groups completely underestimate individuals—individuals who have enormous giving capacity—by not bothering too much with them. Anyone who feels left out or thinks that he or she is seated in a corner of a charity event like an outcast will not forget it and will certainly distance themselves from the organization going forward. That donor will likely take their time, and their donations, elsewhere.

HOW TO SHOW APPRECIATION TO DONORS AND VOLUNTEERS

Those that give financial resources and volunteer their time must be shown great appreciation and thanked properly. Everyone likes to be thanked—and if they are not thanked, they can take offense.

In general, do not worry about thanking someone too much. It would be more prudent to worry about thanking someone too little!

Showing appreciation and thanking someone can be done in several different ways. Keep in mind that some individuals require more thanking than others. Depending on the circumstances, reaching out in a number of different ways to say "thank you" is often required.

Here are just some of the ways a charity can thank its donors and volunteers:

Thank you notes. Thank you notes are essential.

- **Hand-written notes** are never obsolete and should always be sent whenever possible.

- **Typed thank you letters** are also acceptable, as long as they are personalized; adding a short, hand-written note on a typed thank you letter is very effective.

- **Personal e-mails** should not be overlooked or underestimated as an effective and powerful means of communication. In fact, some people prefer e-mail thank you notes. (One benefit to an e-mail note is that it can't be lost: you can have a record of its being sent in digital storage.)

Note: I recommend that *both* a personalized e-mail thank you note and paper note be sent whenever possible.

Press coverage of donors and volunteers. Positive press coverage of donors and volunteers, citing the good work they have provided, is another way of saying thank you. Many of those who have been significant supporters and volunteers like to see their photo or their name mentioned in a newspaper, magazine, or online, and even on TV. If you have control over which photos a publication or media outlet will use, always remember to send attractive photos. No one likes to see a terrible photo of him or herself in a magazine or newspaper! Keep in mind that this type of exposure works to the advantage of the organization as well: positive press helps to build relationships.

Newsletters, annual reports, and website coverage. Donors and volunteers can be recognized in a charity's newsletter, annual report, and on its website. Utilizing these means of showcasing their efforts is another way of showing your appreciation.

Thank you party. Charities often hold small parties to thank volunteers and donors. It is important that budget always be taken into account when planning a party, so that expenses can be minimized.

Honors and awards. Often, charities thank major donors by honoring them at their annual fund-raising events. Awards can also be given to those who have given service above and beyond the call of duty.

Listing on invitations to events. Donors and volunteers are almost always listed on an invitation when they are involved in supporting or working on a specific event. Titles are generally given to donors and volunteers based on their level of giving and/or the work they perform.

Naming opportunities. Rooms, sections of buildings, or entire buildings are often named after major donors. Naming initiatives create wonderful opportunities to acknowledge major donors; by displaying their names to the public, their name lives on and their legacy is honored, and may even inspire further giving to a specific institution. A charity can also name a program after an individual who gives a large sum to fund it. Naming opportunities often have term limits. A charity will need to refurbish a building or refinance a program in the future and term limits on a naming opportunity will allow the building or program in question to be renamed in honor of a new donor who can fund the new project. For example, the name of a building could be available for 25 years, after which time the name of the building might be available to a new donor who plans to renovate it so that it can be used by the next generation.

ANONYMOUS DONORS

Anonymous donors are those who do not want their gifts discussed and who wish to keep their gifts a private matter.

There are many reasons why a donor might prefer to remain anonymous. Many anonymous donors prefer this for security reasons, or they may be uncomfortable with others knowing their level of giving. Then there are those who believe the highest form of giving is anonymous giving.

Regardless of their reasons, anonymous donors are to be honored, respected, and valued, as they play a very important role.

Given the choice, most charities would prefer to list donors and make their gifts public because names often bring in even more names. People sometimes give because they see that the names of friends, neighbors, influential individuals, corporations, and foundations are listed as donors.

The individuals working at a charity must be careful when discussing anonymous donors. Talking about an anonymous donor's gift internally is a delicate matter and should be kept to a minimum.

Please remember that the names of anonymous donors must be kept out of all publications and off the internet.

HOW TO HELP A CHARITY RAISE FUNDS: VOLUNTEER FUNDRAISING

There are many ways to be a philanthropist and contribute to a charity. For people who cannot give very large sums, one of the most valuable ways an individual can contribute is by fundraising for a charity. However, this role is not for everyone. Before you consider asking for donations on behalf of a charity, ask yourself:

Do I believe that the charity I will be fundraising for is well run and doing a good job? Make sure you are comfortable with the charity and that they are well run before you go out and fundraise for them. (Please refer to Chapter 4: How to Choose a Charity.)

Am I passionate and interested enough in the cause to do a good job fundraising? If you are committed to a charity's cause, you will find it easier to attempt to raise funds for them. For example, if your local hospital has asked you to reach out to community members, you will have more success when asking if you truly believe that quality healthcare is needed and that the hospital is vitally important to the community. Your strong desire for good healthcare in the community will come through in your conversations and will absolutely help with your fundraising attempts.

Am I knowledgeable enough about the cause and the charity to be successful? To be a good fundraiser you must be knowledgeable about both the charity and its cause. If you know very little about either, you will be far less successful. Take the time to educate yourself about both before you begin.

Do I have contacts that can benefit the charity? If not, am I comfortable reaching out to new people? Often, someone who has contacts with key people in a community is ideal for this sort of work. However, fundraising can be done by many different people and on various different levels. Reaching out to individuals, foundations, or institutions for donations is serious business.

If you are not comfortable asking others for funds on behalf of the charity, you may prefer to help by making appropriate introductions to a development officer at the charity. Never underestimate the power of making introductions. Just as in business, an individual with strong contacts can be a key asset to a nonprofit organization.

GENERAL GUIDELINES
FOR FUNDRAISING

Once you have determined that fund raising for a charity is a good fit for you, you will need to follow the guidelines below.

Make sure you are educated about the charity and knowledgeable about what you will be asking the funds for. Often, a development officer at a charity can educate you and help you prepare properly before you begin to fundraise. It will be your job to educate yourself about the charity and the specific area you are fundraising for. If you are asked questions about the charity, you will want to be able to answer most of them. Whenever you are asked a question you cannot answer, make sure you refer that question to someone at the charity who can properly respond.

Take the time to learn how to ask. Fundraising is an art form. It also requires proper materials and education. Personal communication is often very important when asking for large donations. Often, fundraising is best done through phone calls or by meeting with an individual in person. Never underestimate the value of speaking with someone or meeting with a person or group. Requests for large sums through the mail or by way of e-mail are often tossed to the side and thrown away. There are exceptions, when some large donors only want to communicate by e-mail or mail, but these cases are rare rather than the rule. Whenever possible, invite a potential major donor to an on-site visit so that he or she can see the actual charity's work in progress. A private site visit can often compel a potential donor to give to a charity.

Remember to be professional and very polite. I have found that an aggressive approach to fundraising does not work. Most people do not want to be pressured into giving funds. Rather, they will give because it is something they believe in and something they want to do.

Be prepared to show paperwork. Most individuals who are asked to make a donation will want to see the charity's official paperwork. Be prepared to mail or e-mail this information. Alternatively, you may want the charity to send official requests directly to individuals; confirm the best way to proceed with the charity before you start.

Make sure that when you ask, you ask for an appropriate amount. Again, a development officer can help you determine the right amount to ask for from an individual, foundation, or corporation. You should never ask for too high of a donation. Ask the advice of the charity and do as they suggest. If someone has just lost a job or is struggling to make ends meet, you should probably not ask for anything at this time.

Don't attempt to raise funds for a charity if you can't accept "no" for an answer. Rejection is all part of the process. A "no" today can be a "yes" tomorrow. Why? A "no" might mean that the individual just needs more information, or more time to decide. It might also mean that now is not the right time in his/her life to give to that particular charity. Do what you can to ensure that, when he or she is ready to give, the charity you represent will be at the top of their list.

If you think you received a "no" because you asked for a sum that was too large, you might want to go back to the individual and ask for a lower amount. You may also want to ask if it would be helpful to provide him or her with more useful information so that they can learn more about the non-profit organization and its work.

Learn humility and how to say "thank you."
Even when the answer is "no," always thank the
individual for his/her consideration. Remember,
you are not asking for yourself; you are asking
for the charity. *This means that you are the charity's representative.* You must be professional and
polite at all times.

Never ask that funds be sent directly to you.
Instead, make sure that all requested funds are
sent directly to the charity. All checks should
be written directly to the charity. Do not accept
a check if it is written to you. Cash and credit
card numbers should be given directly to a
development officer.

**Refer all questions you can't answer to the
director of development or an officer of the
charity**. Major donors will almost always want
to meet and speak with those who run the
operations at a charity. In almost all cases before
a donor gives a large gift, a positive relationship between the donor and charity has been
established.

FUNDRAISING FOR MAJOR GIFTS

An individual, corporation, or foundation that is passionate and very interested in the work of a charity and who has the means to give a major gift should be viewed as a potential major donor.

Developing a friendship and good relationship with a potential donor can take years of cultivation before a gift may actually be received. In certain cases, a potential donor may never give a gift of any significant size.

Often, the President of a charity and its Board Members are the ones a potential major donor will want to communicate with. The development of a trusting relationship is vital between those who run the charity and the potential major donor.

A charity may hold off from asking a potential major donor for a small gift because they want to ask for one large gift. This often happens when a charity is preparing to launch a capital campaign to raise funds to create a new program, renovate an existing facility (in the case of a hospital, museum, educational institution, etc.), or build a new building.

One of the key points of fundraising for major gifts is that *the right person must ask for the right amount at the right time.* In other words, there are often one or two people who would achieve the best results when asking a specific potential major donor for a gift. The right amount must also be asked for. Timing also plays a major role in the success of the receipt of a gift. All of these factors must be figured into the equation before the request is made. A good charity will do its due diligence by researching everything they can about a major potential donor, including what their interests, passions, and giving patterns might be. The organization must then help a potential donor learn as much as possible about the value of his or her potential gift. A trusting relationship between the potential donor and the charity's key people is vital to a successful result. *Just because an individual has wealth does not mean he or she is philanthropic or will be generous to an organization.*

If an organization wants a major gift, they will most certainly have to ask for it. It is highly unusual that a donor will give a major gift without being asked. Quite simply, *if you do not ask, you will not receive*! For example, Richard, a very wealthy real estate developer, was a small donor to a cancer hospital for many years. Every year, he would give $1,000 to the Hospital's Annual Fund. The President of the hospital knew that Richard was very successful and could give more if he chose to do so. Gradually, the President, the Head of Development, and one of the Board Members developed a trusting friendship with Richard. They learned that Richard was interested in giving a major gift but just needed time to sort it all out. A few years into the friendship, the President and a few Board Members were able to take Richard on a tour of the hospital. Richard was so moved by what he saw at the hospital that he decided to give a $10 million gift to create a new wing. The wing was named after Richard and his wife, Mary. The President and Board Members remain friendly with Richard and Mary and greatly value their contribution. In many ways, Richard and Mary are heroes to all those involved with the hospital!

RECRUITING VOLUNTEERS TO A CHARITY

Charities are continually looking for good volunteers to help with a variety of important tasks and duties. One of the ways you can help a charity is by making recommendations and introductions to expand their team of volunteers.

Recommendations and introductions can be done in a variety of different ways. Social events such as dinners, luncheons, cocktail parties, and small or large meetings can all help to facilitate introductions. Some people prefer to meet through phone calls, mail, or e-mail introductions. However they come about, useful introductions are very important to all charities.

If you are interested in helping with the recruitment of volunteers and can make introductions, here are a few points you should consider:

First, learn about the type of introductions that a charity might be looking for. Often, a charity will ask you to make introductions to people you know. You should only agree to do this if you believe you are the appropriate person to make the introduction. If you believe someone else might have better luck with a particular individual, then don't be afraid to say so. *The objective is to bring success to the charity.* Never agree to make an introduction if you are not comfortable doing so.

If you have friends and acquaintances who are interested in a cause and you feel they will make good volunteers, make an introduction.

In general, recommend those whom you know and respect, who show an interest in a cause, and who you believe will be good workers.

If recruiting volunteers is something you really enjoy and you would like to get further involved, make an effort to receive training in recruitment. Most charities, especially the larger charities, should be able to help you get more involved in recruitment or refer you to a program that could train you in this area.

SHOULD YOU START YOUR OWN CHARITY?

Many people with good intentions have started charities, only to have the charity fail. Creating and running a charity is a massive undertaking. It can be more than a full-time job; you will most likely need large amounts of time and financial resources to be successful.

Starting your own charity is a big responsibility. Before you decide to do this, you should be prepared to do a great deal of work and research. Here are just a few questions you will need to answer before taking on this project.

Do you have the financial resources to start a charity? There are many expenses related to starting a charity. Most individuals who start their own nonprofit organization are prepared to personally absorb many of the expenses related to building the charity; a wealthy founder of a charity will often provide large financial contributions in order to ensure its success. Ask yourself if this is something you can do.

Do you have the time to devote to your own charity? In order to get your charity started, you will need to devote a great deal of time and energy to the charity. Be certain that you have the time available to devote to your growing nonprofit organization.

Do you have the proper background to start a charity? Seek advice and try to learn all you can before you attempt to create your own non-profit. Legal advice will be required; starting a charity requires filing for not-for-profit or 501(c) (3) status and adhering to all governmental regulations associated with charitable organizations.

Are you comfortable running a charity like a small business? Starting a charity is serious business and it requires a great deal of financial knowledge, along with commitment, energy, and many other areas of expertise required to keep it up and running. Ask yourself: is this level of commitment and know-how something you are comfortable with?

Will your charity fill a niche or a need? If there are other charities that do the same work to meet a need that you have in mind, and are already succeeding at it, you probably should not start a new charity. You would be better off getting involved with an existing charity, to help further the work they have already started.

Do you believe you have the capability to be successful at fundraising? Is fundraising something you are comfortable with? If not, are you prepared to hire someone to fundraise for your charity? These are all questions you will need to feel comfortable answering before you begin.

Will you have the funds to hire employees as you expand? As your charity grows, you will most likely need help and will have to hire employees. Do you believe that you will have sufficient funds to hire knowledgeable professionals to help with running the charity?

Many small charities have a difficult time surviving because their overhead (as a percentage of revenue) is often very high. In general, annual operating expenses should be *20 percent or less* of annual revenue. Most charities prefer that these expenses be much less. Maintaining this balance is often very difficult for a small start-up charity.

Remember that your charity will be subject to all government regulations and laws. If you are audited, you will need to be prepared. Good accounting and bookkeeping will be essential. Be sure to get legal advice as needed.

Consolidation of 501(c) (3)'s happens quite often. This occurs when a large charity takes over a smaller one that can't make it on its own. Before you begin, make sure that you believe you can succeed!

6

COMMUNITIES BUILT ON GIVING: MODELS FOR SOCIAL PHILANTHROPY

"The test of a civilization is in the way that it cares for its helpless members."

—Pearl S. Buck

N COMMUNITIES THROUGHOUT the United States, philanthropy plays a major role in the lives of many of their citizens. People share their wealth with one another by giving back to their community. Today the most robust, vibrant, and promising cities and towns are communities enriched by philanthropy. Be it a gift of money, or contributions in the form of time and other acts of generosity, citizens who give towards the betterment of the places where they live are working as philanthropists. From large cultural institutions to small-town fundraising initiatives, giving is a part of who we are as Americans—we understand that each of us has the potential to be the architects of lasting change for our friends, our neighbors, and our communities at large.

Tens of thousands of individuals are involved in volunteering for charities. Whether it is for an animal shelter, an antipoverty charity, or for New York City's Metropolitan Opera, people getting together to give and socialize for the benefit of an important cause is a common occurrence in the United States. Many of these same people spend a substantial amount of their leisure time socializing through their charity work. In affluent communities, socializing can revolve around attending charity functions, including dinners, cocktail parties, luncheons, breakfasts, picnics, sports events, polo matches, and musical concerts. The smart charities create events that are stimulating and interesting for those who attend. Participating in charity events can be a priority for the socially conscious person, and is also a way to show that one cares about a cause.

SOCIALIZING FOR A CAUSE

Socializing is often an important part of community giving. Gathering together at a philanthropic event is an exciting alternative to a private party; not only is it a place to socialize, but it is a great way to come together in support of a cause and celebrate the joy and power of giving with others. Support is shared among friends; generally, friends and business colleagues try to support each other's causes to the fullest extent possible. In this way, people learn about new charities and causes, spread the word about an organization's mission, and prompt more giving.

Personally, I have found great fulfillment in charity work, including both the actual work and the socializing associated with that work. My husband and I choose to attend several charity events each month. In many instances, we choose to support a charity event over attending a private party. The events are enjoyable, and we believe in supporting meaningful causes. As often as possible, we try to support not only the causes that we are involved with, but also the causes of others. We make the effort to support the charities of friends and colleagues whenever we can. My husband and I like to learn about new charities, and support those charities that have good leadership, manage finances wisely, and run strong programs.

Of course, socializing at this level requires time and financial resources, so we do what we can. No one is expected to attend every event or support every cause. When our children were young and studying in school, we were much less involved in attending and supporting charity events. We stayed home more and spent needed time with our two daughters. We made sure we were there for them to give guidance, love, and support. But every effort has meaningful results for the community and a cause, and furthers philanthropy in society.

NATURAL DISASTERS FUELING CHARITY

Happy Hearts Fund (HHF) was founded by supermodel Petra Nemcova after she survived the tsunami of 2004. HHF rebuilds safe and resilient schools after natural disasters so that children can continue their educations and communities can return to normalcy. So far, the Happy Hearts Fund has rebuilt 120 schools in nine different countries. Many of the schools that the HHF rebuilds are in South East Asia, including the Philippines.

Like most all other charities, HHF has fundraising activities. In June 2015, one of HHF's Board Members suggested a martial arts/kickboxing fundraiser, and an event was organized in less than 2½ months which raised close to $900,000. The event took place immediately after the Manny Pacquiao v. Floyd Mayweather boxing match. The match drew enormous attention to boxing globally, not to mention the $100 million split between the two boxers. Two days before the event, HHF received a call from Manny Pacquiao's manager saying that Manny was very touched by their mission and was also very devoted to helping his country, the Philippines. His manager explained that Manny was very interested in working with HHF. Manny Pacquiao has promised to help in whatever way he can!

CITIES OF GIVING

Some cities stand out for their active and vital social network built around the cause of philanthropy. Below are just a few of the cities where philanthropy plays an important role in the life of many of its citizens.

NEW YORK CITY

Every year, thousands of people living and working in New York are involved in charitable work throughout the city and its five boroughs. The way New Yorkers give varies; they may serve on nonprofit boards, volunteer their time, give resources, or attend various charity events. Socializing occurs at charity meetings and their respective fundraising events. On almost any given day, there are multiple charity luncheons, dinners, and galas that take place in New York City.

For those who live and work in New York City, a substantial amount of both social and business communication occurs at these events. New friendships are made and old ones renewed. In New York, the social world, business world, and celebrity world all coalesce and come together to support different causes. Often, public officials show their support by attending these events. Philanthropic organizations hold some of the biggest and most exciting parties, including events for the Metropolitan Opera, American Ballet Theater, New York City Ballet, The Metropolitan Museum of Art, the Museum of Natural History, and the Robin Hood Foundation. As one would expect, there is a charge to attend these events, but by attending, individuals socialize with one another while supporting a good cause. Thousands of events occur each year and billions of dollars are raised.

THE METROPOLITAN OPERA (also known as the MET Opera) is a standout example of a 501(c) (3) that has managed to cultivate opera throughout the world. Founded over 125 years ago, the MET Opera is the international home for some of the world's most talented artists, including the world's greatest singers, composers, conductors, orchestra musicians, stage directors, designers, visual artists, choreographers, and dancers. With an annual budget in excess of $300 million, the Metropolitan Opera is both well-managed and fiercely powerful in its drive to deliver first rate opera—the MET Opera premieres some of the most important operas in its repertory, and is host to more than 200 opera performances each year. More than 800,000 people attend performances in the opera house each year, while millions more experience the MET Opera through innovative state-of -the art technology and media distribution. The MET also has a highly successful radio broadcast series, now in its 77th year.

THE HAMPTONS

The Hamptons is a collective name for several beach communities on the eastern end of Long Island. Here, countless affluent New Yorkers, Southern Californians, and Europeans spend their summers vacationing and relaxing by the beach. While often described as the playground of the rich, what many people do not realize is that a very large number of charities hold their events throughout the summer in the Hamptons. These parties begin on Memorial Day weekend and continue right through Labor Day weekend. Getting involved in supporting a charity fuels an exciting social life; charity is very much a part of the fabric and culture of the Hamptons. Each year, more and more non-profits reach out to the Hamptons to seek the support of its summer residents. Local, national and international charities all hold events in the Hamptons.

PALM BEACH

Considered one of the most affluent retirement communities in the world, Palm Beach serves as an excellent model of social philanthropy. Philanthropy is a priority for its citizens, with charity luncheons and dinners occurring almost daily. In fact, some say that the social world in Palm Beach revolves around charitable giving: it is almost a requirement that people be involved in philanthropy on some level. Palm Beach residents seem to genuinely love supporting many different charities. To see a community that collectively makes it a priority to support charitable causes is a wonderful sight indeed!

NANCY GREW up on the East Coast and moved to Los Angeles in her mid-20s. She was well educated and had a career in the fashion industry, which had given her the opportunity to socialize with some of the biggest stars in Hollywood. In her mid-30s she met the love of her life, a prominent doctor. Together they moved and built a life first in the Hamptons, and then in Palm Springs. Nancy loved the idea of giving back and became very involved in philanthropy by first getting involved with the Southampton Hospital in the Hamptons. Giving back has been a very rewarding experience for Nancy. She now is active in charities both in Palm Springs and in the Hamptons. She especially loves her involvement on the Board of the McCallum Theater in Palm Springs. She also loves her involvement with Act for Multiple Sclerosis and will be chairing their gala next year. After her husband passed away, Nancy set up a medical education foundation in honor of him. Through her charitable involvements, Nancy has created many new friendships, and knows that she is leading a most worthwhile life.

LOS ANGELES

Los Angeles, home of the movie industry, is filled with thousands of people who support local, national, and international charitable causes. Celebrities often get involved in supporting causes and can help by bringing visibility to nonprofit organizations. There is no question that celebrities can be very helpful by raising awareness and giving charities their stamp of approval. In addition, celebrities often make major gifts to philanthropy. Outside of the movie industry, there are also thousands of people involved in nonprofits. Just like in any other city, the titans of real estate and finance play a major role in supporting philanthropy. Doctors, lawyers, business professionals, and many others come together to support philanthropic causes. Generally speaking, if you have an interest in a particular cause and live in Los Angeles, you will be able to find a charity that will address the needs of that cause.

SAN FRANCISCO

San Francisco has a very active social group of residents that support the city's arts and cultural institutions. In addition, these citizens support a multitude of other causes. Attending formal fundraising galas for San Francisco's arts, including the ballet and opera, are exciting events for those most philanthropically inclined. The San Francisco Opera, San Francisco Ballet, DeYoung Museum, and the San Francisco Museum of Modern Art all hold major galas that are sought-after events to attend. These cultural institutions also hold major fundraising campaigns.

Those living just outside of San Francisco and who have made their fortunes in the technology field have been instrumental in donating very large sums of money to health and educational institutions. For example, in 2010 Marc Benioff, chairman and CEO of salesforce.com, and his wife, Lynne, gave a $100 million gift to build the new UCSF Benioff Children's Hospital.

7

LEGACY GIVING

"It is every man's obligation to put back into the world at least the equivalent of what he takes out of it."

—ALBERT EINSTEIN

MANY OF THOSE who commit their time and resources to developing meaningful change in their community, their country, or the world, want to make sure that their good works continue after their death. When it comes time to plan our legacies and think about what we want to leave behind, many decide to give back with a legacy or long-term gift. Making the choice to bequeath funds or assets (such as stocks, bonds, or property) to a charity is an important decision, and requires careful planning to ensure that your legacy of giving continues the way you want it to.

Begin by asking yourself which cause, charity, or local institution (such as a school, religious organization, hospital, or cultural institution) you would like to leave a gift to. You can use the guidelines in Chapter 4 to decide which organizations might be of interest.

A will firmly establishes your wishes and outlines how you want your assets to be distributed by establishing *bequests*. Without a will in place, or a lifetime charitable trust established, bequests cannot be enacted. Bequests specifically describe exactly what you want to give, the amount of your gift, and how you want assets to be distributed to the cause or charity in question. There are many different types of bequests.

- A *charitable bequest* establishes what portion of your estate you want to leave to a specific charity or cause, as declared in your will. There are many different kinds of charitable bequests, and you should familiarize yourself with the details of each. The term estate often refers to the sum of your assets, including property, insurance policies, liquid assets, retirement accounts, and so on.

- A *general bequest* is determined based on the overall value of the estate. It is made by deciding on a specific amount, a certain asset, or a percentage of your estate that should be given to the cause or recipient of your choice.

- A *specific bequest* designates an item or property for a specific purpose. Examples include funds set aside to help operate a school, books donated to a hospital library, or instruments donated to an after-school music education program.

- A *residuary bequest* leaves what is left of your assets (known as residue) to a cause or recipient, after other items of the will are addressed.

- If you have a named beneficiary who does not survive you, you may have a *contingency bequest*. This means you will leave the remainder of your estate, if the beneficiary does not survive you, to a recipient, charity, or cause.

It is a powerful feeling to know that after you have passed away you will have done something for the betterment of humanity.

LEGACY GIVING requires the knowledge of a reliable and trustworthy trust and estate law firm. Before considering legacy giving, speak to several experts and learn all you can on the subject. Choose a law firm that you are comfortable with and that you trust to create your legacy giving. This is a very serious undertaking and you and your heirs will want to be pleased with your decision.

A FAMILY LEGACY OF GIVING TO OTHERS

Philanthropic families like the Rockefeller family and the Ford family made a profound decision: they choose to create a format for giving back that would extend beyond their own lifetimes and the lineage of their own families. Since their foundations were established decades ago, generations of people from around the world have benefited from the Rockefellers' and the Fords' choice to think outside of their families' needs. For decades, their foundations have helped to fulfill the needs of humankind.

Founded in 1936, the Ford Foundation was poised to become the largest philanthropic organization in the world by 1947. Over the years, the Foundation went on to provide national and international grants for the betterment of humanity in a variety of areas. To foster creativity and self-expression, the Ford Foundation provided funding for public broadcasting, including a gift to support the creation of Sesame Street. The Foundation also contributed to the growth of great writers with grants to Saul Bellow, Flannery O'Connor, Margaret Mead, and Robert Lowell, among others. Today this Foundation is the second largest one in the world.

The Rockefeller dynasty has been in existence for over a century and sets itself apart with a remarkable family unity that has helped to strengthen the foundation's philanthropic vision. The legacy of giving across the family is quite extraordinary. Spanning the 19th century to the 20th century, starting with father John D. Rockefeller donating over $500 million, to his son, "Junior," who gave $537 million, the total amount of giving in just two generations of philanthropy totaled over $1 billion. The commitment to giving continued through the 2000's, with David Rockefeller giving about $900 million over his lifetime. Because of the Rockefellers, land around the Hudson River and the California redwoods have been preserved, the Rockefeller Center in New York City was created, and major cancer research was nurtured. Additionally, arts and education were given room to grow with gallery space for the Museum of Modern Art in New York City and building space for numerous educational institutions including Spelman College, Vassar College, Harvard University, University of Arkansas, Princeton, SUNY, University of Chicago, Cornell, and Case Western Reserve University.

Rather than set aside the entirety of their financial resources for their children and relatives, the Fords and Rockefellers made a conscientious choice to share their personal resources, thereby planting the seeds of a better future for others and enabling generation after generation to reap the benefits of their gifts.

8
GENERATIONAL GIVING

> *"It takes a noble man to plant a seed for a tree that will someday give shade to people he may never meet."*
>
> —David E. Trueblood

WE ARE THE role models for our children and for future generations. As responsible parents, relatives, and citizens, we bear the duty of serving as *good* role models, to teach future generations the importance of giving back. The world and the society that our children inherit tomorrow will be the one we build and cultivate today!

TEACHING CHILDREN THE IMPORTANCE OF GIVING
THE ROLE OF PARENTS

One of the greatest gifts parents can give to their children is to teach them the importance of philanthropy and helping those in need. Parents can be the greatest teachers. Children listen to their parents and often emulate them. Philanthropy should begin at a young age. The need is there for us to all teach our children about giving back.

Parents should encourage their children to find a cause that is of interest to them. A parent can help their children do this by exposing them to many different causes. Once an interest is found, the parent can help the child choose a well-run charity that they both might get involved with. The process of parent and child choosing a charity and then working together for a cause can be a great bonding experience. By working together, the parent can teach the child many of life's important skills as they relate to dealing with different kinds of people. A child will learn the importance of helping those less fortunate. Family bonding through philanthropy is something that can bring a family closer together over a lifetime. As the child gets older, the initial cause will hopefully remain of interest. A parent who teaches their children about giving back will have instilled very strong values—values that their children can keep throughout life.

CHILDREN WHO ENGAGE PARENTS IN PHILANTHROPY

Sometimes the reverse happens and a child will introduce a parent to a cause. A perfect example is the child who loves animals and asks if the family can adopt a dog or cat from a local shelter. By doing so, the child engages the family in furthering animal welfare. Other times, a child might come home from school with a story about an illness that he or she learned about. The child may be interested in becoming involved with an organization working to help find a cure. This might spur the same interest in the parent. Together, the parent and child can seek out a charity that would address their common desire to be part of the process of finding a cure. Once the right charity is found, the parent and child can become involved together as generational philanthropists. This act strengthens the bond between child and parent while also helping others!

"The greatest of a nation and its moral progress can be judged by the way its animals are treated."
—MAHATMA GANDHI

A NUMBER OF years ago, our daughters decided to get involved with animal rescue. As a child, I never had a pet other than a goldfish. Our daughters, Jacqueline and Elizabeth, first started by rescuing dogs and cats, and as each rescue came into the house, we fell in love with them. Later on, our daughters introduced me to the Southampton Animal Shelter Foundation. Both girls were involved with their junior committee. After becoming acquainted with the Southampton Animal Shelter Foundation and those involved with it, I was asked to chair their annual gala. My first step was to do research on them. Once I was convinced that they were a well-run charity, I said yes to their request. I started by suggesting that they change their annual fundraiser from a cocktail party to a formal dinner gala, thereby enabling the Shelter to raise five to six times more money. I have now chaired the event for four years in a row. As a team, we have been able to raise well over $2 million from the four galas. All of this took hard work. I am grateful to my daughters for introducing me to the Southampton Animal Shelter Foundation. It is now ranked among the top 10 percent of shelters in the United States! Three years ago I was asked to join their Honorary Board and I accepted. Today, I remain very active with the Southampton Animal Shelter and love every minute of my volunteer work with them.

TEACHING THE IMPORTANCE OF PHILANTHROPY IN SCHOOL

There is no doubt that philanthropy and the importance of giving must be taught in our schools, including higher learning institutions. The value of giving must be one of the top priorities of our educational system. Children must learn the necessity of providing help to those in need and they must be taught to care for the underserved.

Thankfully, some educational institutions *do* teach children the importance of giving. However, all educational institutions should require that courses on giving and philanthropy be taught to its students. These courses need to take place in both public and private schools in the United States *and* throughout the world. Children should be involved in community service activities and fundraising efforts, which can include volunteering at soup kitchens, senior citizens homes, and local animal shelters, just to name a few. There should be different volunteer options made available for children. Of course, adult supervision is always required. Basic fundraising activities such as bake sales, toy and clothing drives, penny collections, and raising small amounts of money for little league uniforms are all great ways to get children involved in learning about philanthropy. Children should never be asked to raise large sums of money; the key is to make the act of giving interesting to children so that they will want to make philanthropy a part of their lives.

For example, Mingxing Lin moved to New York City from China with her mother and brothers in 2012 and enrolled at the Emma Lazarus High School on the Lower East Side as a sophomore. She and her mother could not speak English. Desperate to learn and move ahead, she discovered the Learning to Work program given by the New York Mission Society. This program helps over-aged and under-credited high school students graduate. The program's counselors informed her of different college and career options. As her English improved, she realized she wanted to be of help to others. NYC Mission Society helped her get a paid internship in which she was able to help other Chinese immigrants. Her burgeoning awareness led her to run for president of the school's student government, and she won. The 19-year-old graduated in the spring of 2015 and began her college studies at City College in the fall of 2015. Mingxing Lin dreams of becoming a math teacher.

THE ROLE OF RELIGIOUS INSTITUTIONS IN TEACHING PHILANTHROPY

Religion institutions play a major in teaching children the value of philanthropy. No one would argue against the role that most religions play in teaching young people the importance of helping those in need.

THE ROLE OF COMMUNITY AND GOVERNMENT IN TEACHING PHILANTHROPY

Many communities encourage young people to get involved in giving back. All government and community activities that encourage children to participate in philanthropy are of great value.

PHILANTHROPY FOR RETIREES AND EMPTY NESTERS

Retirees, people who have worked all their lives and often very productively, may find that they suddenly have too much time on their hands with not enough to do. After years of leading very busy and productive lives, they often find they would like more to do with their time, so they look for interesting projects to become engaged with.

An empty nester, defined as a parent whose child has grown up and moved along, often feels the same way as a retiree: both frequently come to the realization that they have far too much leisure time and not enough activities.

Often, both retirees and empty nesters can be rather young—in their forties and early fifties—and in great physical and mental shape. Most retirees have been involved in a career all their life, while empty nesters have had the valuable experience of raising a family. Both groups often look for interesting projects to fill their days.

Becoming involved with a charity by volunteering time can be very fulfilling for both retirees and empty nesters, while they can bring a wealth of knowledge to the charity. Both retirees and empty nesters generally have numerous available resources to give to nonprofits. They have worked hard and may have substantial savings. At this stage in their life they may feel that they want to be productive and help those in need.

Retirees and empty nesters can receive great fulfillment through their involvement with philanthropy. They often have highly developed skill sets that younger people do not have. These skills can be invaluable to different charities. Retirees and empty nesters can make excellent board members of charities. They have the time, knowledge, and resources that boards often look for.

Empty nesters and retirees often enjoy the social aspects of their involvement with new charities. They meet new friends and are able to engage in more activities away from their homes.

Philanthropic work can add new meaning to an otherwise rather placid life. For example, Dan was a successful plastic surgeon from Chicago who decided to retire at age 55. After years of performing surgery, he was tired and wanted to enjoy his remaining years. His wife had recently passed away from cancer. Dan was lonely and wanted a way to fill his time. He moved to Florida and started to play golf. He then started to travel. Finally he decided that neither meant much to him. He had always loved the oceans and rivers and decided to get involved with a national water conservation charity, soon becoming fully absorbed in their work. Dan continues to play a little golf and still travels, but now his life has more meaning than it ever had before. He is enjoying his retirement and has even started to date. Dan is leading a fulfilling life while also giving back!

Kay had worked as an executive assistant for a medium-sized company for most of her life. Although Kay was married and then later divorced, she never had any children of her own. When her nieces and nephews were young, she was involved in raising them and had lived a very busy life. Upon retiring at age 65, she found that she still had enormous amounts of energy, but very little to do with her time. So Kay, who lives in Brooklyn, decided to volunteer at a religious school in East New York. To this day, she still works an average of three full days a week as a volunteer at the school. She says her volunteer work has enriched her life enormously. It gives her a reason to get up every day, and she loves helping out at the school. Kay has made many friends with both the parents and teachers. The students love to see her, too. Kay is much happier volunteering her time and is grateful that she does not have to sit around all day with nothing to do but watch television.

Jim, a self-made man living in Chicago, successfully built up a major hedge fund. At the age of 47, Jim started a family foundation which has since grown to be one of the largest in the United States. One day, Jim decided he had had enough of his business. He had earned more than he could ever expect to spend in 10 lifetimes, so at the age of 57, Jim closed his hedge fund and retired from the business. Today he manages his own money and the family foundation. He and his wife, Kate, show their gratitude for his success by giving substantial contributions to major educational institutions. They also give smaller donations to a variety of other charities (almost all of their giving is done anonymously). Jim and Kate have found great happiness through giving!

CONCLUSION

"*We are responsible for the world in which we find ourselves, if only because we are the only sentient force which can change it.*"

—JAMES BALDWIN

LIFE IS A series of lessons. One of these lessons is this: *Hopes must be turned into realities.*

We must make opportunities available to those in need so that they can improve their future.

We are not put on this earth to work with the intention of only giving to ourselves. Good fortune is a gift, and with that gift comes the important responsibility to use our resources to better society. This is *true* personal achievement.

Selfishness does not bring happiness. Few of us will be remembered for the business we created or for how many vacations we took. To feel fulfilled, we must be engaged in helping to make society stronger.

Through the act of giving, we develop a better understanding of *why we are here* and ultimately come closer to reaching self-fulfillment. Understanding the meaning of life can be achieved through the act of giving.

When one shares resources, whether those resources are personal wealth, time, or knowledge, one ultimately comes closer to understanding the meaning of life.

"What we have done for ourselves alone dies with us; what we have done for others and the world remains, and is immortal."

—ALBERT PIKE

TIMELINE:

THE ROOTS OF AMERICAN PHILANTHROPY: GIVING BEFORE THE 20TH CENTURY

I T SAYS A great deal about the American spirit that, before the Declaration of Independence was signed (1776), the telephone was invented (1876), or legislation was passed to pave roads across the country (1893), Americans had already found a way to give back for the betterment of their fellow citizens and communities. From spreading the word about the importance of philanthropy, to making financial gifts that founded universities, to opening charities and libraries, efforts to better the lives of other Americans and the world at large has been woven into the American way of life for hundreds of years.

1630

John Winthrop delivers his speech "A Model of Christian Charity" to the Puritans departing their Native England for North America. In his speech, Winthrop preaches that it is part of the duty of the rich to care for the poor.

1638

John Harvard (1607–1638) contributes to the founding of Harvard University by leaving his library and a portion of his estate in Cambridge, Massachusetts to the University. In 1643, volunteers host what is believed to be America's first fund drive; the first scholarship fund is created; and the president of the university publishes a pamphlet appealing for donations, titled "New England's First Fruits." Through the 1600s and into the early 1700s, gifts to the school, including real estate and monetary donations as well as endowments, help the university thrive.

1702

Cotton Mather (1663–1728) publishes one of the earliest celebrations of the American philanthropic spirit, titled *Magnalia Christi Americana*. Later, he writes *Essays to Do Good*, imploring individuals to give back during their lifetimes and consider leaving an inheritance to others as a legacy.

1704

In New York City, Elias Neau opens a school for enslaved African Americans.

1729

Ursuline nuns found the first orphanage within the present-day boundaries of America in New Orleans, Louisiana.

1731

The country's first lending library is founded by Benjamin Franklin and friends in Philadelphia. Called the Library Company of Philadelphia, the library makes books accessible to citizens from all income levels and encourages the betterment of Americans through the power of reading.

1770

St. George's Society of New York, one of the oldest charities in the United States, is founded in New York City to aid impoverished colonists; other branches opened in Philadelphia, Charleston, across the country, and elsewhere in the world.

1800

The Library of Congress is established by an act of Congress. Later, to help replace books destroyed by British troops, Thomas Jefferson donates one of the finest collections of books in the country—his very own—to the library's collection in 1814. Today, the Library of Congress is the world's largest library, with over 160 million items.

1817

America's first permanent school for the deaf, The American School for the Deaf, is established in Hartford, Connecticut. The school receives an annual grant in 1819, making it the first in America to receive state aid, and is later awarded another grant from the United States Congress in 1820.

1853

New York City's oldest children's charity, The Children's Aid Society, is founded by Charles Loring Brace. A leader in providing welfare services, The Children's Aid Society offered many programs for the first time in the United States, including the forerunner to PTAs, the first free school lunches, first free school dental clinics, and first day schools in New York for disabled children.

1866

Henry Bergh writes a "Declaration of the Rights of Animals" and persuades politicians in the New York State Legislature to pass a charter incorporating the American Society for the Prevention of Cruelty to Animals—forming the first humane society to be established in North America. Soon after, the ASPCA is granted the right to enforce an anti-cruelty law against animals and the work of the ASPCA to prevent cruelty to animals is set in motion.

TIMELINE:

FOUNDING DATES OF WELL-KNOWN CHARITIES, NONPROFITS, AND ORGANIZATIONS AROUND THE WORLD

SOME OF OUR most esteemed national charitable organizations have been serving those in need and working to build a better world for over one hundred years. Below are the founding dates of some of the most well-known and beloved organizations.

1770

St. George's Society of New York

1812

New York City Mission Society (established as New York Religious Tract Society)

1816

American Bible Society

1851

The YMCA, in the U.S. (Young Men's Christian Association)

1853

Children's Aid Society

1860

Boys & Girls Clubs of America

1866

The ASPCA (American Society for the Prevention of Cruelty to Animals)

1877

Fresh Air Fund

1879

The Bowery Mission

1880

The First U.S. Chapter of the Salvation Army

1881

The American Red Cross (established by Clara Barton)

1887

United Way of America

1888

National Geographic Society

1889

Jane Addams Hull House

1892

The Sierra Club

1895

Federation of Jewish Charities of Boston

1899

Veterans of Foreign Wars of the United States

1902

Goodwill Industries

1904

Big Brothers and Big Sisters of America

American Lung Association

1905

The Carnegie Foundation for the Advancement of Teaching

1908

Federated Jewish Charities (now known as Combined Jewish Philanthropies)

1909

NAACP (National Association for the Advancement of Colored People)

1910

Boy Scouts of America

Catholic Charities USA

1912

Girl Scouts of America

1913

The Rockefeller Foundation

American Cancer Society

1916

Acadia National Park

National Park Service

Planned Parenthood's beginnings, in the birth control movement led by Margaret Sanger

1919

Easter Seals

1920

American Civil Liberties Union

1921

American Foundation for the Blind

1922

Shriners Hospitals for Children (first hospital opens)

1924

American Heart Association

1929

The League of United Latin American Citizens

1935

Alcoholics Anonymous

1936

The Ford Foundation

1937

March of Dimes

1940

American Diabetes Association

1942

Oxfam

1944

Heifer International

United Negro College Fund

1946

UNICEF (United Nations Children's Fund)

National Multiple Sclerosis Society

1950

Muscular Dystrophy Association

1960

The Puerto Rican Family Institute

1961

Peace Corps

Amnesty International

1962

St. Jude Children's Research Hospital

United Farm Workers of America

1965

National Endowment for the Arts

1966

National Organization for Women

Reading is Fundamental

1967

The National Park Foundation

1968

Special Olympics

1971

Doctors Without Borders (Medecins sans Frontieres)

1973

The National Gay and Lesbian Task Force (National LGBTQ Task Force)

1974

Ronald McDonald House Charities

1976

Habitat for Humanity International

1977

Save The Whales (founded by fourteen-year-old Maris Sidenstecker II)

1979

Feeding America (established as America's Second Harvest, the Nation's Food Bank Network)

The MacArthur Fellows Program

1980

The Make-a-Wish Foundation

Mothers Against Drunk Drivers (M.A.D.D.)

Alzheimer's Association

1982

Susan G. Komen for the Cure

City Harvest

1985

GLAAD (formerly Gay & Lesbian Alliance Against Defamation)

amfAR (The Foundation for AIDS Research)

1989

The American Indian College Fund

1990

National Council of Nonprofits

1994

William H. Gates Foundation

1995

The American Association of People with
Disabilities

1997

Gates Library Foundation

1998

United Nations Foundation

2005

World Trade Center Foundation, Inc.

REFERENCES

CHAPTER 2

http://www.nytimes.com/2015/06/16/business/charitable-giving-rises-past-prerecession-mark.html

http://givingusa.org/perspectives-on-giving-usa-2014-from-the-chair-of-the-giving-usa-foundation/

http://abcnews.go.com/Travel/guess-nation-generous-world/story?id=27029103

http://www.census.gov/popclock/

https://philanthropy.com/article/The-Stubborn-2-Giving-Rate/154691

https://philanthropy.com/article/Inspiring-People-to-Make-a/152645

CHAPTER 3

http://www.townandcountrymag.com/society/g205/most-generous-families/?slide=2

TIMELINES

http://www.nptrust.org/history-of-giving/timeline/1900s/

FOUNDING DATES OF WELL-KNOWN CHARITIES, NONPROFITS, AND ORGANIZATIONS AROUND THE WORLD

St. George's Society of New York (1770)
www.stgeorgessociety.org

New York City Mission Society (1812)
www.nycmissionsociety.org

American Bible Society (1816)
www.americanbible.org

The YMCA, in the U.S. (Young Men's Christian Association) (1851)
www.ymca.net

Children's Aid Society (1853)
www.childrensaidsociety.org

Boys & Girls Clubs of America (1860)
www.bgca.org

The ASPCA (American Society for the Prevention of Cruelty to Animals) (1866)
www.aspca.org

Fresh Air Fund (1877)
www.freshair.org

The Bowery Mission (1879)
www.bowery.org

The First U.S. Chapter of the Salvation Army
(1880)
www.salvationarmyusa.org

The American Red Cross (1881)
www.redcross.org

United Way of America (1887)
www.unitedway.org

National Geographic Society (1888)
www.nationalgeographic.com

Jane Addams Hull House (1889)
www.hullhousemuseum.org

The Sierra Club (1892)
www.sierraclub.org

Federation of Jewish Charities of Boston
(1895)
www.cjp.org

Veterans of Foreign Wars of the United States (1899)
www.vfw.org

Goodwill Industries (1902)
www.goodwill.org

Big Brothers and Big Sisters of America (1904)
www.bbbs.org

American Lung Association (1904)
www.lung.org

The Carnegie Foundation for the Advancement of Teaching (1905)
www.carnegiefoundation.org

Federated Jewish Charities (now known as Combined Jewish Philanthropies) (1908)
www.cjp.org

NAACP (National Association for the Advancement of Colored People) (1909)
www.naacp.org

Boy Scouts of America (1910)
www.scouting.org

Catholic Charities USA (1910)
www.catholiccharitiesusa.org

Girl Scouts of America (1912)
www.girlscouts.org

The Rockefeller Foundation (1913)
www.rockefellerfoundation.org

American Cancer Society (1913)
www.cancer.org

Acadia National Park (1916)
www.acadiacentennial2016.org

National Park Service (1916)
www.nps.gov

Planned Parenthood (1916)
www.plannedparenthood.org

Easter Seals (1919)
www.easterseals.com

American Civil Liberties Union (1920)
www.aclu.org

American Foundation for the Blind (1921)
www.afb.org

Shriners Hospitals for Children (1922)
www.shrinershospitalsforchildren.org

American Heart Association (1924)
www.heart.org

The League of United Latin American
Citizens (1929)
www.lulac.org

Alcoholics Anonymous (1935)
www.aa.org/pages

The Ford Foundation (1936)
www.fordfoundation.org

March of Dimes (1937)
www.marchofdimes.org

American Diabetes Association (1940)
www.diabetes.org

Oxfam (1942)
www.oxfam.org

Heifer International (1944)
www.heifer.org

United Negro College Fund (1944)
www.uncf.org

UNICEF (United Nations Children's Fund)
(1946)
www.unicefusa.org

National Multiple Sclerosis Society (1946)
www.nationalmssociety.org

Muscular Dystrophy Association (1950)
www.mda.org

The Puerto Rican Family Institute (1960)
www.prfi.org

Peace Corps (1961)
www.peacecorps.gov

Amnesty International (1961)
www.amnesty.org

St. Jude Children's Research Hospital (1962)
www.stjude.org

United Farm Workers of America (1962)
www.ufw.org

National Endowment for the Arts (1965)
www.arts.gov

National Organization for Women (1966)
www.now.org

Reading is Fundamental (1966)
www.rif.org

The National Park Foundation (1967)
www.nationalparks.org

Special Olympics (1968)
www.specialolympics.org

Doctors Without Borders (1971)
www.doctorswithoutborders.org

The National Gay and Lesbian Task Force
(National LGBTQ Task Force) (1973)
www.thetaskforce.org

Ronald McDonald House Charities (1974)
www.rmhc.org

Habitat for Humanity International (1976)
www.habitat.org

Save The Whales (1977)
www.savethewhales.org

Feeding America (1979)
www.feedingamerica.org

The MacArthur Fellows Program (1979)
www.macfound.org

The Make-a-Wish Foundation (1980)
www.wish.org

Mothers Against Drunk Drivers (M.A.D.D.)
(1980)
www.madd.org

Alzheimer's Association (1980)
www.alz.org

Susan G. Komen for the Cure (1982)
www.komen.org

City Harvest (1982)
www.cityharvest.org

GLAAD (1985)
www.glaad.org

amfAR (The Foundation for AIDS Research)
(1985)
www.amfar.org

The American Indian College Fund (1989)
www.collegefund.org

National Council of Nonprofits (1990)
www.councilofnonprofits.org

William H. Gates Foundation (1994)
www.gatesfoundation.org

The American Association of People with
Disabilities (1995)
www.aapd.com

Gates Library Foundation (1997)
www.gatesfoundation.org

United Nations Foundation (1998)
www.unfoundation.org

World Trade Center Foundation, Inc. (2005)
www.911memorial.org

JEAN SHAFIROFF, philanthropist, is considered to be at the vanguard of a new movement of modern philanthropists. Jean's philanthropy goes beyond financial contributions and includes the gifts of extensive time and knowledge. Through her work she encourages and seeks to empower all individuals to become philanthropists so that they can build the fulfillment of giving into their lives.

A volunteer fundraiser, leader, and spokesperson for several charitable causes, the spectrum of Jean's philanthropic work includes improving the lives of underserved populations, women's rights and well-being, health care, animal welfare, and resources for children in need, in addition to other causes. Jean serves on the boards of New York City Mission Society, New York Women's Foundation, French Heritage Society, Couture Council (Museum of the Fashion Institute of Technology), Jewish Board of Family and Children's Services (20+ years),

Southampton Animal Shelter Honorary Board, and Southampton Bath & Tennis Club's Charitable Foundation.

Jean has been widely recognized and featured in numerous publications, including *The Wall Street Journal*, *Gotham Magazine*, *The New York Times*, *New York Social Diary*, *Avenue*, *Hamptons Magazine*, and *The Huffington Post*, among others.

Jean works closely with the multiple causes she supports. Each year she chairs numerous galas and hosts events benefiting numerous not-for-profit organizations. She is particularly well-known for her leadership in raising money for many charities, including the Southampton Hospital, New York City Mission Society, New York Women's Foundation, and Southampton Animal Shelter. Jean has been honored by several organizations including the New York City Mission Society, Youth Counseling League, Jewish Board of Family and Children's Services, Surgeons of Hope, the Ellen

Hermanson Foundation, Pet Philanthropy Circle, and Animal Zone International.

Jean holds an MBA from the Graduate School of Business at Columbia University and a BS in physical therapy from the Columbia University College of Physicians and Surgeons. She has worked both in public finance and private partnerships on Wall Street. Prior to that, she was a physical therapist at St. Luke's Hospital in New York City. Jean is married to Martin Shafiroff, an investment advisor, and together they have two daughters, Jacqueline and Elizabeth, who share their mother's interest in charitable causes. Jean and her family reside in New York City and Southampton.